Nobin Chandra Das

Legends and Miracles of Buddha, Sakya Sinha

Nobin Chandra Das

Legends and Miracles of Buddha, Sakya Sinha

ISBN/EAN: 9783743311541

Manufactured in Europe, USA, Canada, Australia, Japa

Cover: Foto ©Lupo / pixelio.de

Manufactured and distributed by brebook publishing software (www.brebook.com)

Nobin Chandra Das

Legends and Miracles of Buddha, Sakya Sinha

LEGENDS
AND
MIRACLES OF BUDDHA,
SAKYA SINHA

PART I.

Translated from the Avadan Kalpalata of Bodhi-Sattwas,
Of the great Sanskrit Poet

KSHEMENDRA.

BY

NOBIN CHANDRA DAS, M. A.

OF THE BENGAL PROVINCIAL SERVICE, TRANSLATOR OF RAGHU-VAMSA.

Calcutta:

PRINTED AND PUBLISHED BY JADU NATH SEAL
HARE PRESS:
46, BECHU CHATTERJEE'S STREET.

1895

To

H. G. COOKE ESQ., I.C.S.

Who has taken a most generous interest

IN

The Author's Humble Works,

This Book is Respectfully

DEDICATED

BY

His most Loyal Servant

Nobin Chandra Das.

KRISHNAGHAR,
4, September, 1895.

PREFACE.

IN offering these pages to the public, my object has been to bring to their notice and specially to that of European scholars, some of the sublime sentiments and noble precepts which hitherto lay hidden in the undiscovered Sanskrit Buddhist works of India.

The high principles propounded by Buddha, Gautama or Sákya Sinha, which shaped the religion of most of the Asiatic nations, emanated from the doctrines and philosophy of the Indian Aryans. *

---

* Mr. R. C. Dutt, the translator of the Rig-Vedas, observed, "The cardinal tenets of Buddhism, the doctrine of *Nirvána*, and the doctrine of *Karma* were directly derived from Hindu ideas and Hindu practices, and Buddhism was the offspring of Hinduism." Buddhist Text Society's Journal Vol. I. Pt. II.

Buddhism flourished in India as a religion, and as a system of ethics, or philosophy, under the powerful kings of Magadha, and owing to its similarity with the religion and ethics of the Vedas and the Upanishads, became in the lapse of time assimilated and merged in the latter. It lost its character as a separate religion and regained its original niche in the many-sided and all-comprehensive structure of Aryan or Bráhmanical philosophy, just as its great teacher, Buddha, himself was admitted into the Hindu Pantheon as an incarnation of the Deity, the highest position to which a man can aspire.*

Naturally enough, the same doctrine, propagated in the countries beyond Arjyávarta or India,

---

* "It may, I think, be confidently affirmed that Vaishnavas and Saivas crept up softly to their rival and drew the vitality out of its body by close and friendly embraces, and that instead of the Buddhists being expelled from India, Buddhism gradually and quietly lost itself in Vaishnavism and Saivism."

Sir M. Williams' Buddhism p 170.

"Though the profession of Buddhism has for the most part passed away from the land of its birth, the mark of Gautama's sublime teaching is stamped ineffaceably upon modern Bráhmanism and the most characteristic habits and convictions of the Hindus are clearly due to the benign influence of Buddha's precepts " Preface to Sir Edwin Arnold's "Light of Asia."

where the people had no definite religion of their own, took deep root, as a religion pure and simple, grew and flourished extending its wide branches and soothing shade to the farthest limits of Asia.

It is a pity that most of the Buddhistic works on religion and philosophy did not survive the ravages of time and the bigotry of foreign conquerors in India. The colossal Buddhist-Sanskrit work *Bodhi-Sattva Avadán Kalpalatá* written by Kshemendra, the great Sanskrit poet of Káshmir, narrowly escaped a similar fate. It was lost in India, but has been recovered from "a monastery in Tibet by the enterprising scholar and traveller, Mr. Sarat Chandra Das. Kshemendra wrote 107 legends of the *Bodhi-Sattvas* in graceful Sanskrit verse, and his son Somendra wrote another tale to complete the auspicious number 108." *

---

* Mr. R. C. Dutt, B. T. S. Journal Vol. I. Pt. II.

My brother, *Sri* Sarat Chandra Das, C.I.E., gives the following account of the work, which is now being published by the Asiatic Society of Bengal, in the Bibliotheca Indica Series :—
"I visited the ancient libraries of Sakya, Samye and Lhassa, which were filled with original Sanskrit works taken from India. The library of Sakya is a lofty four-storeyed stone building of great size, erected about the 12th century, A.D. It was here that the monumental work of Kshemendra, called "Avadán Kalpalatá," was translated into Tibetan verse by the order of

Kshemendra, known for his learning, as "Vyása-Dása" (follower of Vyása) was born on mount Tripura, in Kashmir. His father's name was Prakáshendra. He studied under such teachers as Abhinava Gupta and Bhágavatácháryya Soma-Páda. He was the author of numerous works on history, philosophy, religion, romance, and a variety of other subjects. The names of 36 of these have been discovered. *

Though born and brought up as a Hindu, he held in veneration all that was sublime in the tenets of the different sects of the Vedic and Brahmanical religions, and of Buddhism as well, as

---

Phags-pa, the grand hierarch who converted the Emperor Khublai to Buddhism……. As regards the *Dalai Lama's* library at Lhassa, it is considered the largest of all the libraries in Tibet. It was here that I obtained Kshemendra's Avadan Kalpalatá." Ibid.

* These are :—अमृत-तरङ्ग, अवसर-सार, औचित्यविचार चर्चा, चमक-ज्ञानकी, कला-विलासकाव्य, कविकण्ठाभरण, चेमेन्द्र-प्रकाश, चतुर्वगसंग्रह, चारु चर्या, चित्र भारत नाटक, दर्पदलन, दशावतार-चरित्र, दान-पारिजात, देशोपदेश, नीतिकल्पतरु, नीतिलता, पद्य कादम्बरी, पवमान पञ्चाशिका, बुद्धचरित Life of Buddha, बृहत् कथामञ्जरी, बोधिसत्त्वावदान-कल्पलता (Bodhisattvávadán Kalpa Latá), मुक्तावली काव्य, मुनिमत मीमांसा, राजावली, रामायणकथासार, ललित रत्नमाला, लावण्यवती काव्य, वात्स्यायन सूत्रसार, विनय-बल्ली, वेताल-पञ्चविंशति (Vetál Panchavinsati), योगाष्टक, शशि-वंश, समयमातृका, सुवृत्त-तिलक, सांख्यसर्वोपदेश, महाभारत मञ्जरी ।

appears from his works, "Dasávatár Charita" (The Ten Incarnations), "Muni-Mata-Mimánsá," and the present, "Avadán Kalpalatá."

He was undoubtedly a devout admirer of Buddha, whom he believed to be an incarnation of Vishnu and accorded a rank, superior to Brahmá and Indra :

" Him followed Brahmá and the gods,
Whom all the worlds adore."
Sri-Gupta, St. 15 p. 48.

He effectually brought about a reconciliation between Bráhmanical religion and Buddhism, which, though not antagonistic in the main doctrine, shewed divergencies in external form, and ran counter to each other, during the ascendency of the Mágadha kings.

The " Ráj-Tarangini " of Kalhan Pandit, makes mention of Kshemendra's historical work " Rájávali." Kshemendra wrote his " Samaya Mátriká " in the reign of king Ananta (25 Local Era) and his " Dasávatár Charita " in 41 L. E. when king Kalasha ruled in Káshmir.*

---

* "एकाधिकेष्टं विहितचत्वारिंशे स कार्तिके ।
राज्ये कलश-भूभर्तुः काश्मीरे'वच्युतस्सव: ।"
The above account has been taken from the " Viswa Kosha."

I undertook to translate into English verse 4 out of the 108 cantos of this colossal work, for the Journal of the Buddhist Text Society of India, edited by *Sri* Sarat Chandra Das and my object will be fulfilled if, in spite of the imperfect garb in which they have been put by me, the intrinsic beauty and sublimity of the sentiments contained in them, receive the attention they deserve, at the hands of indulgent readers, and induce abler scholars to take up the work of translating the whole of the book and thereby throw a flood of light on the religion and doctrines of Buddha.

The story of *Eka-Sringa* * is based on the legend of Risyasringa of Válmiki-Rámáyana, and romantically describes how a young man brought up by his father in the solitude of a forest from his birth, and ignorant of the fair sex, could not resist the impulse of love, owing to innate desires and

---

* This legend has been translated into Japanese, by Mrs. Fujiye, a distinguished lady of Kioto, Japan, and published in the Journal of the Temperance Society of Kioto. The lady writes thus in the preface of her translation :—"I am very much interested to read this sweet and beautiful poem which is translated by Nobin Chandra Das M.A., from an ancient Sanskrit Scripture and appeared in the Journal of the Buddhist Text Society of India. I translate this into Japanese poetry and let readers taste how sweet it is."

habits of former lives. It strikingly illustrates the principle of transmigration of the soul, which is the key-note of the Buddhistic faith.

The legend of *Rukmavati* illustrates the principle of self-sacrifice with a view to relieve the distress and save the life of others.

The story of *Jyotishka* describes how he was saved from the womb of his dead mother by the miraculous power of Buddha, and how he renounced the world under the oppressive rule of *Aját-Satru*, king of Magadha. It teaches the efficacy of true faith and devotion.

The legend of *Sri-Gupta* inculcates the sublime lesson of Forgiveness, and *ahinsá* (अहिंसा) which Sir Edwin Arnold puts as follows:

"Kill not -for pity's sake—and lest ye slay
The meanest thing upon its upward way."
Light of Asia, B. VIII.

It narrates how Sri-Gupta, at the instigation of an anti-Buddhist, made a plot to poison Buddha by inviting him to a feast, and how the calm forgiveness and mercy of that Enlightened Being converted him into a devout follower!

"The Lord saved Sri-Gupta from spite and crime
And shewed how mercy conquers e'en a foe ;
And thus he taught Forgiveness' rule sublime,
To free his followers from the world and woe." p. 59.

I offer my grateful thanks to the Revd. A. Tomory, M. A., of the Free Church Institution, Calcutta, who most generously revised my translation of the first two legends, and thereby encouraged me in the arduous task, which I had so rashly imposed upon myself.

KRISHNAGHAR,
17th February, 1895.   NOBIN CHANDRA DAS.

CONTENTS.

EKA-SRINGA.

Jasodhará's love for Buddha (st. 3-5 . .	2
Buddha's reply to the Bhikshus (6 and 7) . .	2
Story of Nalini, princess of Benares and her visit to Eka-Sringa's hermitage (11-24) . .	3
Eka-Sringa and Nalini meet (25-35) . . .	5
Eka-Sringa innocently tells his father Kásyapa about the change in his mind (47-54) . . .	9
Kásyapa's anxiety for his son and his denunciation of the fair sex (58-62)	10
Nalini's second visit and success in winning over Eka-Sringa (64-69) . . . , .	12
Eka-Sringa's marriage and ignorance of wedded life (70-74)	13
He becomes king of Benares and appears as Buddha at a future birth (78-80	15

RUKMAVATI.

Rukmavati's compassion for a woman at child-birth (st. 6 to 11)	17
She offers her flesh to save her (12-15) . .	18
She was born again as Satyavara and felt anxiety to feed hungry birds (20-27)	20
Satyavrata sacrifices his life to save a tigress and her new-born cubs (28-46)	21
His birth again as Buddha (48-50) .	24

Jyotishka.

Buddha's prophesy about Subhadra's son (st. 4 to 8)	26
A kshapanak's attempt to falsify it (9-16)	27
Subhadra causes his wife's death 17-22)	28
Buddha saves the child born of the dead mother and names him Jyotishka (23-33)	29
King Bimbisára took the boy and brought him up (34-37)	31
Subhadra took Jyotishka to his home (38-43)	32
Jyotishka's prosperity 44-52	33
Oppression of King Ajat-Satru (53-60)	33
The effects of good rule and evils of tyranny (61-72)	36
Worthlessness of worldly prosperity (73-78)	39
Jyotishka renounced the world and followed Buddha (79-84)	40
Efficacy of true faith and devotion (85-96)	41

Sri-Gupta.

A kshapanak's denunciation of Buddha (st. 6-10)	46
Sri-Gupta's plot to poison Buddha 11-17)	47
A Bhikshu's anxiety, hearing the plot 18-21)	48
Buddha allays their fears 22-25)	49
Miraculous power of Bodhi-Sattvas (26-36)	49
Sri-Gupta sees Buddha and becomes his devout follower (37-41)	52
Story of Anupama, queen of Benares and the peacock 43-58)	53
The queen fell into temptation (60-65)	56
Her attempt to poison the peacock fails and she dies of remorse and shame 66-71	57
Spite, folly and passions are the direst poisons (72-74)	58
Doctrine of mercy and forgiveness (76-78)	59

EKA-SRINGA*

A BIRTH STORY OF BUDDHA, SÁKYA SINHA.

———:-o-:———

E'V'N in the mind that's free from fear,
Ardent desire has oft-times grown
Out from habits of former births
Luring the senses, to pleasure prone :
The lotus flower thus burgeons forth
From roots deep sunk in fertile mire,
Attracting by her fragrance sweet
The busy bees in humming quire.

2

In days of yore the blessed one
Resided in "the Banyan Grove"
Of Sákya's city. Him around,
The Bhikshus came and spoke in love :—

---

* Translated from the 65th canto of Kshemendra's Avadán Kalpalatá.

3

'Now thou from earthly pleasures safe
Art changed in mien and freed from care,
Ev'n Yasodhará, in palace rich,
Entranced stands at sight so fair.

4

Her beauteous limbs, with jewels decked,
Tremble like ripples in the brook ;
Holding in hand a dish of sweets
E'er lovingly she courts thy look.

5

With downcast mind she knows no cheer
But sighs for a glance of thy face ;
She droops, as fades the lily flower
When waning moon withdraws her grace.'

6

So spoke the monks : great Buddha heard
And thus bespake them with a smile ;
His crimson lips and pearly teeth
Adorned a face all free from guile :—

7

Yasodhará not first to-day
With charms doth captivate my heart ;
So did she in her former life
Lure me with cakes and Love's sweet art.

8

Good king Kásya in Kási town
In olden times held royal sway,
As with a goad subdued his foe,
With fame as fair as lunar ray.

9

Vows he performed to get a son
Only a girl to him was born,
Her name Nalini : She alone
Became the fruit of Plenty's horn.

10

So year by year the maid grew up,
No brother or sister her youth did share ;
At last the king sought council wise
And to his friends told his despair :—

11

"My sovereignty, without an heir
Is like a lofty widespread tree,
Affording shelter unto all
Yet worn and cankered inwardly.

12

"Nalini, my sole darling child,
Is on the threshold of her youth :
To wed her to a husband meet
Would free me from my care and ruth.

13

"For, who can keep his daughter long
Or unburned hold a burning wick ?
She causes her dear father care :
'Tis better she be married quick.

14

"But she, born princess of this realm,
A noble of it may not wed,
And so unto some foreign land
When Hymen bids she 'll turn her head ;—

15

"Unless a kindly Fate decree
That foreign prince shall hither come,
And of my throne shall partner be
And of my girl the mate become."

16

There lives on Gangá's sacred bank
Sage Kásyapa of royal blood,
Lone in a peaceful hermitage
Built just beside the rolling flood.

17

A thirsty hind drank in the stream
And she became the mother proud,
Of Kásyapa's saintly son,
Renowned by the admiring crowd.

18

From day to day she gave him suck ;
The hermit-father owned his son,
Who from the one horn on his brow
His name of Eka-sringa won.

19

The child grew up religiously
To piety he was devote ;
Little he cared for earth's affairs
His soul was free from every mote.

20

Him did king Kásya wish to gain
As husband for his daughter dear,
For such a union would prevent
Of his realm's fall the dire fear.

21

The ministers conferred a while
Then to the king their counsel told ;
It was to let his daughter roam
At will, beside the hermit's wold.

22

The king agreed, and with his leave
The maid went to the wood to roam :
It was a brave exploit for her
To seek the youth near to his home.

23

The black-eyed maiden in the wood
Looked beautiful in frolic gay,
Her lithesome form and grace excelled
The creepers moved by Zephyr's sway.

24

She culled the flowers and chased the flies
Her presence sweet did rouse the deer,
The hermit's son their flight did see
And to discover the cause drew near.

25

He paused when first his eyes did rest
Upon the black-eyed maiden there,
For in his woodland home till now
He ne'er had seen a maiden fair.

26

And through him then her eyes did flash
A current of celestial fire ;
The poor boy did not understand
The rushing feeling of desire.

27

But on her face he gazed and gazed
And wondered what the fair might be,
Was it a god or vision rare,
That with these eyes he now did see?

28

And she in turn at him but glanced,
Then sank her head upon her chest,
A rising blush crimsoned her cheek
And shamed the necklace on her breast.

29

With love she quivered in every nerve
And love-sweat moistened her blue-black hair,
And her amorous bosom heaved and sank ;
Then her bespake the hermit fair : —

30

" O, hermit blest, if hermit thou be,
Thrice-blest are those wood-roaming deer,
That in thy favour live and bask
And in thy presence know no fear.

31

" Thy beauty doth mankind refresh
Even as a draught of nectar rare ;
Compared to thee, ascetic looks
Of other hermits dull appear.

32

" The smooth dark cluster of thy locks
Set off with ferns and flowers gay,
Looks like the peacock's varied plumes
Displayed at sight of cloud's array.

33

" The white beads* hanging o'er thy breasts
Which round appear like fruit of *bael*
Enchant the leaping fawns: to charm
The pure in heart they never fail.

34

" A leafy zone of *munja*, † bright
As sparks of sacrificial fire,
Girdles thy waist and clings to thee,
And with its clinging joy inspires.

35

"Oh, tell me, pray, where thou dost dwell?
There surely must be found great bliss,
The lotus in thy foot-print springs
Yellow and white for sunbeams to kiss."

36

And as she heard, the maid perceived,
Of love how witless the youth appeared ;
So maiden's shame she put aside
And sweetly glanced at him, nor feared.

37

Then gently to the enraptured sage
The princess spoke in accents coy :
" My hermitage is over there
Come there with me and see my joy."

38

So said the maiden with a smile
Tempting the youth to go her way ;
Offered him cakes with camphor mixed
Soothing as music at cool of day.

---

* String of pearls thought to be a rosary.   † A kind of grass.

39

With honeyed cakes and amorous talk
And lover's lore which charms the ear,
The princess by her wiles allured
The hermit, artless as the deer.

40

" Show me thy grove," the hermit cried
And closed his eyes in ecstacy,
Feeling her arms around his neck,
Enraptured with love's rhapsody.

41

She led the way, he followed her
Drawn by magnetic cords of Love :
Into her chariot grand she climbed
Inviting him with her to rove.

42

Seeing the horses he held back,
For hornless stags they seemed to him ;
And 'twere a crime for him, he thought,
Hind-born, to whip and drive his kin.

43

He would not mount, so all alone
The maiden homewards drove her pair.
The loving youth in mind she bore
And told her sire his story rare.

44

The king in council him bethought
Of means to win the hermit young
By guile, but not by force, for fear
The hermit father's wrath be stung.

45

So he devised a floating stage
Of boats decked like a hermitage,
On which the lovely princess fair
Might carry off her lover sage.

46

The while Eka-sringa's father wise
Observing his dear son neglect
His sacred duties to perform,
Thought Love to blame for this defect.

47

And asked him, "Son ! what ails thee, then ?"
The youth replied with deep drawn sigh,
Which gently shook like Zephyr's breath
The quivering twigs of plants close by :—

48

"Father, I saw in yonder grove
By Gangá's side, a hermit sure ;
Whose face was like the spotless moon
Whose eyes became my cynosure.

49

"His neck, and hands, and waist were girt
With beads reflecting rainbow-hues.
Why, father, is it that I lack
Such ornaments that grace infuse ?

50

"The music of his loving voice
Still vibrates in my inmost heart ;
The hum of bees or cuckoo-note
Compares not with his artless art.

51
"The bark that round his graceful form*
He wore, was white as Gangá's foam ;
My barky covering now doth seem
Compared with it as black as loam.

52
"He pressed my cheek to his lotus-face
And in his arms he me embraced ;
His tender lips spoke passioned prayers,
As I in his sweet clasp was laced.

53
"And ever since I've had no peace
Nor shall, till I see him again ;
Sweet balmy sleep from me repelled
By thoughts of him I seek in vain.

54
" For day and night nought else I see,
But the outline of his face divine ;
Nor can I think of sacred rites
While for his absent form I pine."

55
The wise old hermit understood
That Love had claimed his only son,
His round of meditation left
And thought on what could now be done —

---

* The hermit-boy, used to wear bark, took the silk dress of the princess to be fine bark.

56

"Alas, this youth born of a hind
Has fall'n wounded by woman's eye!
Innocent he of snares and wiles,
Has been trapped by a woman sly."

57

His love-struck son he then addressed,
And told the cause without alloy,
That he had been oppressed in heart
With love and lover's seeming joy.

58

"It was no hermit-boy," he said,
" But maiden fair that thee allured ;
In her there lies the fang of love,
Whose poisoned sting cannot be cured.

59

" They who are struck by woman's glance,
And captured by her painted eye,*
And thrilled with pleasure at her touch,
Shall in this world's dire prison die.

60

"For woman's beauty, lightning-like,
Corruscates with a dangerous play,
Over man's miseries and pains
Sheds fitful flash, then dies away !

---

* Refers to the custom of painting the eye with black dye *(anjan)*.

61

"Woe unto him who cannot flee
From woman, child of vanity,
Mysterious elf of Ignorance,
Bringer of ruin and insanity!

62

"Happy are they who live in peace,
In solitude, and suffer nought
From darting glance of woman's eye,
With pain and peril ever fraught."

63

In such a strain the father spake
To free his son from Love's strong chain;
But his fiery soul was kindled now
With Beauty's flame: so words were vain.

64

And when, as was his wont, next day
His sire to gather sticks was gone,
The love-sick youth beheld the maid,
Returning to her quest half-won.

65

The princess, with her train of maids
Shining as creepers with blossoms gay,
Beheld with joy the youthful sage
Fair as cupid, on Love's hey-day!

66

With sweet red lips she then did speak,
"Come to my hermitage's shade,
Where *Kalpa* trees with mellow fruit
Do bend." He followed, as she bade.

67
He saw the floating hermitage
Of boats, o'er-hung with jewels bright,
And golden foliage and flower,
And entered in with great delight.

68
The floating grove him meanwhile bore
To holy Kási down the stream,
As man, unknowing, is borne away
By earthly thoughts that come in dream.

69
Thus to the Royal Court he came
Adorned with jewels of wondrous size ;
He fancied Heaven, by sages sung,
Had come before his mortal eyes.

70
The monarch then, rejoiced in heart,
Bestowed the princess on the youth ;
Her necklace trembled as she walked
Round fire, plighting her bridal troth.

71
The nuptial fire with off'rings burnt ;
And with her gentle hand in his,
The bridegroom thought he yet did stand
Beside the sacred fire in bliss.

---

* Practised his vows as an ascetic, still ignorant of wedded life.

72

The king with height of festive joy
Honoured the son, who lingered still
With him intent on vows, then took
His bride back to his forest rill.*

73

The Mother Hind beheld her son
Roam with his wife in wooded glade ;
Endowed with speech by her hermit-mate,
She asked him "whence did'st get this maid ?"

74

He bowed to her and fondly said : —
"This beauteous person is my friend,
Whose friendship and sweet company
Before the sacred fire I gained."

75

The mother found the simple youth
Still ignorant of wedded life ;
To where the hermit-matrons lived,
She led her son and his fair wife.

76

The matrons thus addressed the youth :
" This is the partner of thy life,
The sharer of thy pious vows."
And so he knew her for his wife.

77

The hermit old then told his son
The duties of the married life ;
Advised by him the youth repaired
To the king's palace with his wife.

78

The old king placed him on the throne,
And sought for peace in solitude ;
The youthful sovereign ruled the land,
Receiving tithes from chiefs subdued.

79

The pomp of regal power and wealth
Stirred not the tenor of his mind ;
But in old age he left the world,
Leaving his family-cares behind.*

80

This Eka-sringa (the one-horned) am I,
Yasodhará is Nalini, my wife ;
Her charms surviving from former birth
Grace even now my peaceful life.

81

Thus *Jina* did his former life recite ;
The Bhikshus heard in wonder and delight.

---

* Became a hermit in old age.

RUKMAVATI*

A BIRTH STORY OF BUDDHA, SÁKYA SINHA.

MY halting tongue fails to declare
    Heroic deeds both great and fair,
Of those whose lives relieve Earth's woe,
Whose wounds, like *lotus*, glory wear. †

2

In times of yore Lord Budh proclaimed
How men with him true peace might share ;
He wandered' mongst Kaivarta tribes,
Thence did to solitude repair.

---

* Translated from the 51st Pallava of Kshemendra's Avadán Kalpalatá.

† Wounds resemble red lotus. The Goddess of prosperity is said to dwell on lotus flower. Martyr's bloody wounds are glorious,

3

To adore and pay him homage due,
Great Indra came, lord of the sky;
A radiant smile played o'er his face;
What secret doth beneath it lie!

4

To wond'ring Indra, Budh declared
The reason of that heavenly look:
"' Twas memory of former life,
That of my face possession took.

5

" The sudden joy which flushed my mind
Was due to reminiscence old,"
So said the Lord, and then began
The story of his life to unfold :—

6

" Rukmavati, a noble dame,
Lived in Utpalávati town;
Her poorer neighbours shared her wealth,
For Mercy claimed her as her own.

7

" She saw one day a wretched hag,
Through hunger desperate and wild,
Glare eager, like a monster dire
To tear and eat her new-born child.

8

"The dame was moved by pity sweet
To stop the crime, and thus did speak:
'Alas! the love of self doth lead
Man into sin when will is weak.

9

" 'This frantic woman may not be
E'en for a moment left alone;
Or else the infant will be killed
And torn asunder skin from bone.

10

" 'And if I take the child with me,
While home I swift for food do fly,
The mother, half-dead even now,
Will from starvation surely die.'

11

" One moment stood she in suspense,
Uncertain still which way to go;
She fell into a trance, and found*
The way, to save the world from woe!

12

"Then swift as thought, with glistening knife,
She cut for food her rounded breast;
Unmoved she offered it to the hag
Who lay by hunger still oppressed.

13

" The wretch ate it, and spared the child;
The fame of this devoted act
Spread o'er the earth, and Indra came
In Bráhman's guise to ask the fact:—

14

" 'Fair lady! when thou gav'st thy breast,
Was aught unwilling then thy mind?'
To him replied the noble dame,
Who to weak flesh was wondrous kind:

---

* In the principle of self-sacrifice.

15

"'When I cut off my mature breast,
My mind was then all free from doubt ;
Now for this virtue let me be
A man, and womanhood hence scout.'

16

" So spake the lady sweet and good,
And in a moment ceased to be
A woman mere, and was transformed
Into a man, right fair to see !

17

" Just at that time by Fate's decree,
The great king Utpalákshya died
Without a son to fill his place :
To choose a king the ministers tried.

18

" As Rukmaván, the new-formed youth,
Possessed both gifts and graces great :
And so on him did they bestow
The rank and power of royal state.

19

" This virtuous youth long ruled the state
With power and great prosperity ;
Time came at last for him to die,
For no man lives to eternity.

20

" His next life was as merchant's son :
Now Satyavara was his name ;
Who for his inborn guilelessness
And charity, was known to fame.

21

"His pensive mind e'er dwelt upon
Creation's miserable lot ;
E'en sufferings of helpless birds
Did not escape his anxious thought.

22

"In penance then he cut himself,
And on the burning ground he lay ;
Around his bleeding frame did fly
The carrion birds, on him to prey.

23

A savage bird flew down and perched
Upon his head, and with bill stout
Pecked at his right eye, and then tried
To dig the ball completely out.

24

"The youth unflinching lay in pain,
In mind still resolute and firm,
And calmly to the bird he said,
' Eat, from me thou wilt get no harm.

25

"'The frame of clay devoid of worth,
Destined to perish when life is run,
Is only worthy when it leaves
Something of good for others done.

26

"'This body vile which works but ill
Is scarce for preservation fit,
Attains its end, if sacrificed
For wretched mortal's benefit.'

27
" E'en as he spake, a flock of birds
Rapacious settled on the corse,
Completed quick their loathsome work
And picked his bones without remorse.

28, 29
" In his next birth a Bráhman's son
Was he, Satyavrata by name ;
Learned, and celibate, and kind,
Lived in the wood with spotless fame.

30, 31
" Like saintly souls, did he possess
Wisdom and noble birth and love ;
So he through thought and solitude
In time his passions rose above.

32
" He dwelt within a hermitage,
Clear and sublime his soul did grow,
Until at last a test supreme
Unto his mind his faith did show.—

33
" A tigress lay and moaned in pain
Expecting soon the birth of young :
The saint resolved to give his life
To save the cubs from being wrung.

34
" To give their mother timely food,
The holy man quite fit to die,
Prepared to be the tigress' prey
By love of creatures lifted high.

35

" In seven days her cubs were born,
The pain set up a thirst severe :
To quench the same she thought to kill
Her offspring young that lay quite near.

36

" The saint perceived the struggle keen
Between the love of cubs and self
Proceeding in the tigress' mind,
And said, holding his life as pelf :—

37

" 'Alas! that this poor thirsty beast
Should wish her new born cubs to slay,
Thus selfishly to save herself
And with their blood her thirst allay !

38

" 'For pain does breed such selfishness
As otherwise we should eschew,
And even bonds of motherhood
Are snapped by anguish sharp and new.

39

" 'But 't were a sin that she should eat
Her offspring young ; so I betime
Will offer my body, to slake
Her thirst and save her soul from crime.

40

" 'For fame immortal them awaits
Who freely give their bodies up
For others, and despise the flesh,
Which drops like dew from lotus-cup.'

41

"Of pointed wood a dirk he made
And pierced his sacred throat and thence
The blood did rush, while he himself
Fell prone the tigress' thirst to quench.

42

"The mind of one who is truly great,
Made soft and pure by mercy's flow,
Still graceful by relieving pain,
Stands not aloof at sight of woe.

43

"And so he was the tigress' prey—
For soon she tore his body bare ;
Her claws' gashes blazoned, as it were,
The noble victim's glory rare ! *

44

"Like Mercy incarnate, unmoved
He bore the tigress' wounds severe,
As Love and Forbearance endure
Faults ; or Faith, practices austere. †

45

"Under the tigress' weight and claws
His body soon faded away,
And with the hair that stood erect
Looked like the moon with shooting ray !

---

* The bloody gashes on his body are likened to heraldic emblazonments or inscriptions, or record of the great exploit.
† Practice of austerities is possible when one's faith is strong.

46

" He calmly viewed the tigress, mad
With drink of blood from out his breast ;
His soul then mused on next sojourn,
And took at throat, a moment's rest. *

47

" The tigress then moved him around
Bashfully glanced as in carouse,
And thrilled delight into his heart
As if she wished to be his spouse.†

48

" Self-possession unflinching e'er,
A mind bent on relieving woe,
And fame which flows like virtue's stream,
Mark out the pious here below.

49

" Soon all of him had disappeared,
But not until the earth had quaked
As if in fear, when this great soul
Passed into sleep, a while unwaked.

50

" And then he came again as *Jin*'
For merit of his former strife,
And cruel death which he endured ;
Thus Satyavrat received new life."
And thus the sage concluded then
" This was the reason of my smile,
For I remembered former lives ; "
And Indra admiring gazed the while.

---

* It is believed that the soul passes by the throat into the brain before its final exit from the body.

† The movements of the tigress after she was satiated with his bood, delighted him, by consciousness of his having done his duty.

THE STORY OF

JYOTISHKA.*

THE evil which o'ertakes the pious,
  Brings blessings in its train ;
And bliss forebodes to wicked folks
  The sure approach of pain.—
The midnight gloom displays the ray
  Of light-emitting bowers, †
And day which gladdens Nature's face,
  The owl's eye-sight o'erpowers.

2

In Rájgriha, the famous town,
  Where Bimbisára reigned, ‡
One Subhadra lived, and by thrift
  A happy living gained.

---

* Translated from Kshemendra's Avadán Kalpalatá, Canto IX.

† Luminiferous creepers, known to Sanskrit poets as *Osadhi* or *Jyotirlatá*, shine to better advantage when the night is dark.

‡ Vidmisára is called Bimbisára in the Váyu Purán, and is the same king of Rájgriha (in Magadha) in whose reign Gautama Buddha was born in Kapilavástu, and his son Ajátsatru is the powerful king, in the eighth year of whose reign, Gautama died.
                                    R. C. Dutt's Ancient India.

3

To all philosophy a foe,
  He loved, by folly led,
The Kshapans, who with priestly craft
  The country had o'erspread.

4

His wife, Satyavati by name,
  In time did pregnant grow,
And looked as flush as orient sky
  With rising moon a-glow.

5

Lord Buddha, then in Kalandak
  Lived in a lonely wood,
One day to Subhadra he came
  To ask for mouthful food.

6

Subhadra and his goodly wife
  With reverence him adored;
To tell the future of the child
  Unborn, they him implored.

7

"Your son," he said, "will prosper here,
  And gain heavenly power,
And follow in my path to attain
  Salvation's happy hour."

---

* Kshapan or Kshapanak is a term applied to Bráhman priests by Buddhists.

8

So said the Lord and went his way
  Towards his lonely wood ;
Just then Bhurik, a Kshapanak,
  Walked to the door and stood.

9

Subhadra then expressed to him
  All that the Lord had said,
The Kshapan heard with feigned distrust,
  And grew with envy mad.

10

Versed in astrology, he viewed
  The starry spheres o'erhead,
And in his mind he found as true
  What Lord, the Budh had said.

11

Then thus he thought within himself
  "All that Budh said was true ;
What else of truth can I divine
  His wisdom to undo?

12

"Should I by word of mine confirm
  His power and teachings wise,
The Kshapans will lose people's love
  And *Sramanas* will rise." *

13

Reflecting thus in mind he spoke
  Through jealousy and spite ;
" What the arch-pretender said
  Is myth and false outright.

---

* Buddhist monks.

14

" How can a man attain on earth
    Power and bliss divine ?
It may be, he will wander forth
    A wretched life to pine.

15

" One who is struck by penury,
    To help whom none would care,
Becomes a beggar all his life,
    A *Sraman's* lot to share.

16

" O master of the house, I see
    If thou hast faith in me,
The child, if born, will surely be
    A source of woe to thee."

17

The Kshapanak then went away ;
    Subhadra, left in gloom
Be-thought of ways to kill the child
    Still in its mother's womb.

18

When drugs used for the end desired,
    Were found to be in vain,
To person pressure was applied,—
    The mother died in pain.

19

The wretched husband took the corpse
    To Sitávan to burn ;
The Kshapanaks were greatly pleased
    The evil news to learn.

20

" Ah," they cried, " what the sage foretold
    Has truly come to pass ;
The quick'ning of the ill-starred child
    Has killed the dame, alas !

21

" Is this the child's power divine,
    And this, his bliss on earth ?
A wanderer's life ended here
    In death, before his birth !"

22

Thus they spoke in jest and glee,
    The rumour spread like fire ;
A mighty crowd assembled round
    The dame's funeral pyre.

23

Buddha, by all the world adored,
    To all creation kind,
Saw with a smile all that had passed,
    And thus thought in his mind—

24

"Ah, how the guile of wicked men
    Puts out the inward ray
In simple folks and makes them blind,
    As clouds o'ercast the day.

25

"The Kshapans with pretensions bold
    To shun all ills betime,
Have led the foolish man astray
    And plunged him into crime."

26

So thought the Lord, by pity moved,
  And with his *Bhikshu*-train, *
Hastened to where on dismal pile
  The lady's corpse was lain.

27

The great king Bimbisára heard
  The Lord's arrival there,
And followed by his ministers
  Did to the place repair.

28

When lo, a child on lotus borne
  Bright as the orient sun
Came bursting forth the corpse's womb,
  With blazing fire o'errun.

29

When none did dare to take the babe
  From out the rising flame,
There rose from all the crowd around
  A doleful cry of shame.

30

One Jivaka, a valiant knight
  By *Sugata's* command †
Sprang forth, and rushed into the flame
  And held the child in hand.

---

* Crowd of ascetics who followed Buddha.
† *Suga ta, Thathágata, Jina* are appellations of Buddha.

31

At the calm and all-soothing sight
   Of *Jina*, for the while,*
The fire had cooled like sandal-paste
   E'en on the horrid pile.

32

At sight of child alive and fresh
   Amid the burning flame,
The Kshapanaks were mute as death
   And stood aloof in shame.

33

To Subhadra who still remained
   Lost in amazement wild,
The Lord who brings relief to all
   Thus spake, "Take this, your child."

34

Subhadra still stood in suspense
   Uncertain what to do,
Looked at the face of the Kshapans
   To know their biddings too.

35

"This child, of funeral fire born,
   Thou take not home", they cried,
"That house is doomed to utter ruin
   Where this elf shall reside."

---

* Ruddy flame is compared with red sandal-paste.

36

The foolish man thus led astray
    Declined to take the boy;
The king obeyed the Lord's command
    And took the child with joy.

37

Bright as a star the child came forth
    From out the fiery light;
The Lord himself gave him the name
    Of Jyotishka, "the Bright."

38

In the king's palace he grew up;
    And in the course of time,
His uncle on maternal side
    Came home from foreign clime.

39

His sister's fate and nephew's birth
    He learnt with grief profound;
To Subhadra in rage he turned,
    With crime he charged him round.

40

"By faith in Kshapanaks," he cried,
    "O knave, what hast thou done?
Hast murdered thy dear loving wife,
    And hast forsook thy son!

41

"A fool with no sense of his own
    Like goblin, laughing though,
By others' incantations led,
    Does mischief as a foe.

42
"If thou, from palace takest not
Forthwith the child that's thine,
For murder dost thou run the risk
Of forfeiture and fine."*

43
By rebuke taken thus aback,
And brought to sense by fear,
Subhadra took his boy straight home ;
The king rejoiced to hear.

44
Subhadra died in course of time ;
And Jyotishka, his son
Grew rich in wealth and rose in power
Like as the noon-tide sun.

45
He spent his wealth in charity,
Devoted all his mind
To *Buddha, Dharma* and *Sangha,* †
So dear to human kind.

---

* It would appear that under the Buddhistic rule, capital sentence was not resorted to, in cases of murder, under the well-known principle of अहिंसा. The original sloka stands thus :

"अघ्नैव न गच्छामि यदि राजगृहात् मृतम्
तत्ते स्त्रीवधमुद्दिश्य कारयाम्यर्थ-निग्रहम् ॥ ४२"

† The Buddhistic triad. *Buddha* is supreme enlightenment, *Dharma* is practice of virtue and *Sangha* is the congregation of ecclesiastics. Some scholars are of opinion that *Sangha* represents actual creative power deriving its origin from the union of the essence of *Buddha* and *Dharma*.

46

His aim of life was to attain
  Piety and virtue pure ;
He gave rich stores of precious things
  To *Bhikshus*, ever poor.

47

Prosperity from gods on high
  Unto his home did flow,
As streams descend from snowy peaks
  Into the sea below.

48

And e'en the Lord before whose eye
  Both grass and gold are one,
Deigned from him presents to accept
  By his devotion won.

49

By virtue and piety he gained
  Of cloth divine, a pair.*
Which for its milk-white purity†
  Might with his fame compare.

50

The cloth wet after bath, one day
  To dry in sun was spread,
When it was wafted by the wind
  Just o'er the monarch's head.

---

* He got a pair of cloth of celestial make.

† In Sanscrit poetry, fame is described as white and pure (Vide st. 8, p. 2, & 69, p. 38).

51
The king admiring stood at sight
  Of cloth so nicely made;
Its heavenly splendour served to throw
  His wardrobe into shade.

52
The monarch with his presence, graced
  Jyotishka's stately home;
It looked like heaven, here below
  With glitt'ring spire and dome.

53
The virtuous king in after time
  Was murdered by his son,
Aját-satru, who mad with greed,
  Usurped his father's crown.*

54
His tragic death untimely closed
  His blessed golden reign,
The prince now ruled and brought around
  Impiety's evil train.

55
The matchless wealth of Jyotishka
  He viewed with jealousy,
And thus addressed that worthy man,—
  "My father fostered thee :

---

* We get a historical fact here that Ajat-satru caused the death of his father, Bimbisára, and ascended the throne of Magadha.

56

"Thou art my brother thus by law
   So share thy wealth with me ;
Or else to get my lawful rights
   To fight I challenge thee."

57

Jyotishka thus addressed by him,
   With guile and mischief fraught,
Gave up to him his house and all,
   And elsewhere refuge sought.

58

Prosperity, so blest and bright,
   Chose after him to run,
With all her bounteous store and train,
   As light doth follow sun.

59

She shunned the king and followed still
   Jyotishka's humble life,
Though thrice forsaken, in her love
   Like a devoted wife.

60

The king's rapacity and crime
   O'erspread the country round ;
Jyotishka thus thought in his mind
   With pain and grief profound :—

61

"A gracious king, as father kind,
   To all his people dear,
Now dwells in memory alone,
   On sinful earth so rare !

62

"Oh, for the king whose rule benign
  Makes nightly sleep secure,
On whom the people may rely
  As on their father, sure!

63

"The rich abound as rank as reeds,
  Like gems, the wise are few;
Rarer than nectar is the man
  Whose heart is pure and true.

64

" How few are they whose noble souls
  Are free from vanity,
Untouched by guile, sincere and just,
  From earthly folly free.

65

"The prince by greed and malice led,
  Does revel now in crime;
Wicked *Kali*, through people's sin,
  Has come before his time!*

66

" That glorious king is now no more,
  The friendly sun is set!
His son now reigns in gloom supreme,
  With all its ills beset.

---

* *Kali* is the fourth period or *Yuga* of world's age, when people become wicked.

67

" The wicked, oft-times, serve as friends,
   To good men, dead and gone,
By setting off their pious deeds,
   Against acts of their own.

68

" So must I leave this world for good,
   In such a monarch's reign,
Where he and evil times combine,
   Life is a source of pain.

69

" When virtuous king rules on the earth,
   Men live a blameless life ;
Then merit thrives ; and faith and love
   Ennoble household, wife ;
Then wealth and fortune fairly earned,
   And fame like moon-beam pure,
Make people happy and content
   From peril e'er secure.

70

" And then Religion's glorious tree
   Grows and o'erspreads the land.
Unshaken by oppression's blast,
   Untouched by tyrants' hand ;
'Tis nourished by a nation's wealth
   And faith without alloy ;
Yields virtue, piety, as its fruits
   For people to enjoy.

71
"*Kali*, as youthful tyrant dire,'
  Let loose his evil train ;
Revolt, unrest and funeral fire
  Have marked his wicked reign.

72
"Man's mind is dull, and love is faint,
  Happiness, past her youth ;
For me no pleasures of the earth
  Have relish aught in sooth.

73
"Riches and land, house and attire,
  And servants, children, wife,
Like maladies which know no cure
  Do cling to man through life.

74
"Wherever Riches sheds on man,
  Her fitful summer-ray,
There burns the fire of quenchless thirst
  Consuming life away !

75
"The life-long flow of earthly wealth,
  Like ocean's briny store,
Can scarce assuage the thirst of man—
  Ambition knows no shore.

76
"Could plenty stop the discontent
  Which haunts the rich on earth,
Man would not come to life again
  Through pain of frequent birth.

77

"Away with wealth, the fertile cause
  Of discord, fight and woe!
Farewell, false pride and favour low
  Which princes can bestow!
Away enjoyment and its want,
  That are with perils rife!
'Tis best for man, in evil times,
  To lead a recluse life.

78

"Good company's ray does scarcely gleam,
  In gloomy times of sin,
The pious then seek rest and peace
  In solitude unseen."

79

Jyotishka then renounced the world,
  Reflecting thus in mind;
Misfortunes open wisdom's eye
  While they confound the hind.

80

He gave up all, and followed Budh
  Salvation to attain,
For one who's tied by Lucre's chains
  Seeks happiness in vain.

81

So when a drake in Mánas' lake*
  Longs for to live and swim,
The nether earth, with muddy pools,
  Has charms no more for him.

---

* Lake Mansarowara, north of the Himalayas, the abode of the gods.

82

When pleasure's fiery thirst is choked
    With folly's blinding smoke,
And when contentment's nectar soothes
    The souls of peaceful folk ;
Then Fortune with her drink and mirth
    And fair one's flitting charm,
To those retired and happy few
    Can do nor good nor harm.

83

Unwearied, with the Lord as guide,
    He walked life's journey through,
And so he led a wanderer's life
    In quest of quietude true.

84

Enlightenment he thus obtained
    As *Bodhisattwa* * wise
The *Bhikshus* saw and asked the Lord,
    Who thus to them replies :—

85

" Man reaps the inevitable fruits
    Of actions of his own, —
The deeds which in his former births
    As potent seeds were sown.

---

* One, whose soul has become enlightened and purified by practice of virtue. Buddha-hood is the last stage of enlightened existence.

86

" When Bandhumán held royal sway
  In Bandhumati town,
There lived a man named Anangan
  Of great wealth and renown.

87

A preacher of enlightened mind
  Once to that city came
For sake of virtuous people there,
  Bipasyi was his name.

88

"The sage was followed by *Bhikshus*
  Thousands, three score and two,
Anangan welcomed him with joy
  And bowed with reverence due.

89

" Three months he entertained the sage
  With all his means and might;
The king invited him as well
  With reverence and delight.

90

" The worthy citizen and the king
  Each with the other vied
In honouring the guest with treat
  To suit their wealth and pride.

91

" With jewelled umbrella and flags
  And elephants arrayed
The king adored the saintly guest,
  Anangan saw dismayed.

92

Great Indra saw and pitied him
  And from his heavenly store,
Bestowed on him enormous wealth,
  The *Blessed* to adore.

93

Anangan then adored the Lord
  With riches thus obtained,
Eclipsed the bounty of the king,
  And lasting fame attained.

94

With flowers, perfumes, and precious gems
  Resplendent as the sun
And moon in full, and *kalpa* fruits,*
  He adored the Blessed one,
Whom *Indra's* queen devoutly fanned
  With *chámars* gently swayed. †
He put, by such devotion rare,
  The king's display to shade.

95

By faith unflinching in the saint
  He purity did gain,
And in Jyotishka, bright as sun,
  Has come to life again.
And so from earthly turmoils free
  He moves at last in peace with me."

---

* *Kalpa*-tree of Paradise which yields fruits according to the desire of the gods or the pious.

† The hair of the tail of *chamari* deer (Yák) is used in fanning kings and great personages.

96

So said *Jina*, whose wisdom pure
    Has lit the world, all through,
And thus he taught his followers
    Devotion's value, true.

SRI-GUPTA*

A MIRACLE OF BUDDHA, SAKYA SINHA.

1

THE pious with compassion melt
　E'en for one that has wrought them harm;
Their coolness soothes the heat of spite,
　Their calm doth cruelty disarm.

2

There lived in Ráj-gir glorious town
　Sri-Gupt' in times of yore,
Whose hoard of treasure justly vied
　With Mammon's † boundless store.

3

For virtue little would he care
　By riches puffed, and vain,
Oppressed the pious and viewed the good
　With rancour and disdain.

---

* Translated from Kshemendra's Avadán Kalpalatá, canto 8th.
† The wealth-god Kuvera is the Indian Mammon.

4

For Fortune showers her smiles on men
　Who are crooked, hard and fell
And hollow, sounding like *conch*-shells,
　Wherein she loves to dwell.*

5

A wicked Kshapanak, his kin
　A libertine at best,
Once came to him and recklessly
　In secret him addrest :—

6

"Budh, claiming worship from the world,
　As omniscient renowned,
Now dwells on *Gridhra-kuta* hill †
　With *Bhikshu*-host around.

7

"No power nor merit, aught for good,
　Can one discern in him ;
The mob has raised him to the skies
　And praised as lord supreme !

---

* This refers to the legend that Lakshmi, the goddess of wealth, arose out of the ocean, which abounds in shells and pearls. *Conch*-shells are used as trumpets.

† Gridhra-kuta (Vulture Peak) is one of the 5 hills, which surrounded Ráj-griha in Magadh (Behar). The Chinese traveller Fa-Hian states that "the 5 hills formed a girdle like the walls of a town." According to Turnour, the Páli annals of Ceylon describe them as Gijjha-kuto, Isigili, Webháro (Baibhár), Pándáwo and Wepullo (Vipula Giri of the Mahá Bhárat). Cunningham's Ancient Geo. India. p. 463.

8

"He e'er repeats what others said,
   And judgment he doth lack,
As one who treads the public road
   Afraid to miss the track !

9

"His penances and vows are traps
   To draw the good astray :—
The crane stands silent on one leg
   To assure his finny prey !

10

"So let us now expose his wile
   That charms and leads away
A foe-man ev'n, unused to guile,
   The dupe of earth and clay."

11

Sri-Gupt' by fate and *karma* led,*
   His evil counsel heard ;
And to commit a dreadful crime,
   His reckless heart was stirred.

12

A secret pit he dug and filled
   With burning coal and wood ;
And to invite the lord he went,
   To a treat of poisoned food.

---

* The act-law of previous births, which regulates man's affairs in his present life (Vide Jyotishka, st. 85 p. 41.)

13

The Lord, whose omniscient eye
    Saw through the deepest guile,
Accepts the invitation false,
    And pities with a smile.

14

The fire and poison sorely grieved
    Sri-Gupta's goodly spouse;
The husband feared she might betray,
    And shut her in the house.

15

Great Budh who knew all that was meant
    Left for Sri-Gupta's door;
Him followed *Brahmá* and the gods,
    Whom all the worlds adore.

16

Meanwhile Sri-Gupta's fiendish plan
    Soon spread all o'er the town—
For crime will out, despite one's care
    To hide and keep it down.

17

A follower then approached the Lord,
    Fell prostrate at his feet,
Sore frightened at the murd'rous plot,
    And spoke in accents sweet:

18

"Do thou, O Blessed, shun this man
    So falsely meek, and dire,
Who deeply plots against thy life
    With poisoned food and fire.

19

"For who can trust a wicked man
 Though looking fair and true?—
A razor fine with shining blade
 Still cuts the entrails through!

20

"The wicked hardly bear to hear,
 The praise of pious folks;
What charms the good, doth pain the vile,
 Whose malice it provokes.

21

"If thou, whose effluent rays have oped
 Creation's lotus-eyes,*
Dost fall, to this Ráhu, a prey, †
 Eternal gloom will arise!"

22

The Lord heard this with least concern
 And thus replied with smile,
Its ray serene dispelled the fear
 Of murder, dark and vile:—

23

"In burning flame, or poisoned food
 Is aught for me to fear?
E'en crime can do no harm to those
 Whose minds no malice bear.

---

* Buddha is compared to the sun, whose rays light the world, and open the petals of the lotus flower.

† Sri-Gupta who plotted against Buddha's life is compared to Ráhu (the shadow) which is said to swallow up the sun and cause an eclipse.

24

"Can fire, or venom injure him
  Whose calm dispassionate mind,
By meditation mollified,
  Is e'er to creation kind ?

25

"On spiteful folks ambrosia sweet
  May work as venom dire,
And flower on them as thunder act
  Or sandal-paste, as fire !

26

"And e'en a *Bodhi-sattva* true
  Though born in bestial frame,
To save by love, and kind to all,
  Is e'er secure from flame.

27

"*Kalinga's* king in olden time
  Impelled by hunter's greed
Set fire to woods in *Khanda-Dvip*
  To catch the antelope breed.

28

"A partridge young was grieved to see
  The burning of the wood ;
And gaining "*Bodh*" through pity great
  Unhurt, the flames withstood.*

---

* He attained the virtue of *Bodhi-sattva* (enlightened). The fire ceased near him, after burning the rest of the forest. Bodh is the attribute or essence of *Bodhi-sattva*.

29

"So one whose soul is free from spite
 Has nought in earth to fear;
The wond'rous power of *"Sattva"* wise
 Be pleased once more to hear:—

30

"In season of a dreadful drought
 Which scorched a hermit's wold,
There lived a hare, *Bodhisat*-born
 Generous, wise and old.

31

"He found the hermit, about to die
 With hunger sore opprest,
And in his mind as firm as rock,
 In pity him addrest:—

32

"'Do thou, O Sire, feed on my flesh
 And save thy body pure,
For then it will enable thee
 To practise virtue sure.'

33

"So said the hare and threw himself
 Into the glowing fire
Despite the hermit's anxious care
 To stop the venture dire!

34

"His wondrous power of *"sáttvic"* will
 The spreading fire did stay,
And turned the wood into a lake
 With smiling lilies gay.

35

"He rested on a lotus blue,
  His form refulgent grew ;
Adored by sages, all around,
  He taught Budh's tenets true.

36

"No fire can burn nor venom touch
  The *Sattv' of Bodhi* pure."—
So said the Lord and walked his way
  Unto Sri-Gupta's door.

37

Soon as he stepped the threshold o'er,
  The scene all changed, and lo,
The fire-pit turned into a pool,
  With lotus red a-glow !

38

Sri-Gupta saw the Lord enthroned
  On lotus-blossoms gay ;
His mind cleared at the sight, he knelt
  And thus began to pray :—

39

"Forgive, O lord, this wretch, whose life
  Ev'n now with sin runs o'er,
He that is lost in folly's gloom
  Doth need thy pity more.

40

"By evil nature drawn astray
  No hope is there for me ;
Salvation ne'er can I attain
  Except by grace of thee.

41
"A dainty dish with poison mixed
　　I did design for thee ;
That pois>n in repentence' shape
　　Now turns and tortures me."

42
With heart so sad, and tearful eyes
　　He wept, and suppliant prayed ;
Kind *Budh*, with *Bhikshus* him around,
　　Thus pitied him and said :—

43
"Weep not, good friend, nor think that we
　　Are hostile e'er to thee ;
No poison injures pious men
　　From malice-poison free.*

44
"King Brahma Dutt in olden time
　　Ruled in Benares town ;
His queen, Anupamá, for grace
　　Obtained a wide renown.

45
"Once in the royal park, there crowed
　　A peacock in his pride ;
The queen from palace heard his voice
　　That echoed far and wide.

46
"The sound like that of woodland reed
　　Did fill her heart with glee ;
And curious, she asked her lord,
　　What music it might be.

* Poison of ill-feeling.

47

" 'A pretty peacock', said the king,
  'There sings in yonder grove ;
His clear resounding voice, you hear
  From o'er a league, my love.'

48

"To shew to her the pretty bird
  The queen entreats her lord ;
The king yields to her pressure sweet,
  With many a loving word.

49

" 'This bird of varied plumes', he said,
  'Tis hard to catch and see,
Still for thy sake, I'll try my best
  To bring it home to thee.'

50

"The king's command spread o'er the land ;
  Unnumbered hunters hied
With traps and rods ; to catch the bird
  Alive or dead, they tried.

51

" One, held in thraldom by his wife
  Enchained with strong love-ties,
Doth oft commit the grossest wrong,
  And hardly trust his eyes.

52

"Uxorious men by wives held low
  As footstools, oft resign
Their honor, fame, and common sense,
  At blind-fold Cupid's shrine.

53

"The nets and traps, by hunters spread
  At every step were torn
Or shunned by that proud peacock-chief,
  With wondrous powers born.

54

" The hunters tried with all their might
  But failed to catch the bird ;
The peacock saw their wretched plight,
  And was by pity stirred.

55

" 'Ah, these poor hunters that have failed,
  To seize and capture me,
Are sore afraid of their king's wrath,'—
  So thought the bird, still free.

56

" The peacock then consoled his foe, *
  And flew to palace gate,
And followed slow the anxious king
  Into the *harem* straight.

57

"The gentle bird lived there for long
  Loved by the royal pair,
And as a beauteous faithful pet,
  Was served and fed with care.

58

"Oft in the emerald-tower he danced
  In pride of cloud-like blue,
His charming variegated plumes,
  Displayed the rain-bow-hue !

---

* The hunters, who wanted to seize him dead or alive,

59

"And when the king in greed of power
    Marched out to foreign lands,
He placed the bird—his favourite charge
    In fair Anupam's hands.

60

"The queen in absence of her lord,
    In youth and beauty's pride
Forgot her virtue, faith and self,
    O'erpowered by passion's tide.

61

"In Cupid's fight with Faith, she fell
    To youthful Love a prey;
Fair Modesty, a woman's pride,
    Took fright and fled away.

62

"How fickle, full of mischief, wild
    Is fair-eyed maiden's glance!
Her dark long eyes which reach the ear,
    Look guilefully askance.

63

"The world, like ocean full of sharks,
    Is play-ground to the fair,
Her charms infatuate the man
    And poison unaware.

64

"Her mind more tender than a bud,
    More crooked than a saw,—
Its nature, who can understand?
    It strikes the good with awe.

65

"Whoe'er resigns himself in love
  To erring faithless wife,
Doth swallow, witless, as it were
  A cold fine-bladed knife!

66

"The faithful bird, endowed with speech
  In palace used to stay;
He proved an eye-sore to the Queen,
  An obstacle in her way,

67

"'This bird will tell the king my tale
  And then I'm doomed for e'er;
O! what a fall is this in me!'--
  She thought in dire despair.

68

"'The peacock full of sense, and wise
  Knows all that happened here;
Now that I've sinned, e'en life-less things
  O'erpower me with fear!'—

69

"So thought the queen, and poisoned food
  She mixed to kill the bird;
Is aught which women cannot do
  By evil passions stirred?

70

"The bird ate it; the poison dire
  Caused him no harm nor ill;
It raised the splendour of his plumes,
  The hues grew deeper still!

71

"The bird was safe ; remorse, and fear
   Lest he disclose her crime
Preyed on her mind ; and so she drooped,
   And died before her time.

72

"The deadly venom wrought no harm
   To the honest bird so good ;
The purity of pious souls
   Unpoisons pois'nous food !

73

"True poisons causing death and ill
   Are passion, folly, spite ;
Buddha, and Sangh, Dharma and truth *
   Yield nectar, life and light.

74

"True poisons arise from folly's sea, †
The passion-snakes beget them too ; ‡
The wild of spite yields poisons dire ; §
Whence else arise such poisons true ?

---

* *Vide* foot notes to st. 74.

† Poison is said to have arisen from the Ocean, when it was excessively churned by the *Devas* (gods) and *Asuras* at the mandate of *Siva*. The direst poison is that which arises from the ocean of folly (*moha*) or worldliness with its ignorance.

‡ The direst poison is also that which emanates from the passions, compared to venomous serpents.

§ The direst poisonous drugs are those which grow in the wilderness of spite or ill feelings.

75

"Sri-Gupta had made a fiery pit
  E'en so in former life,
On mischief bent ; that pit was born
  To punish him as wife." *

76

So said the Blest by mercy moved
And looked Sri-Gupta in the face ;
The glance lit up his inmost soul
Diffusing unspeakable grace !

77

Sri-Gupta saw the happy light
By this communion with *Jin*',
And thought of three-fold refuge pure ; †
The sight of saints saves man from sin.

78

The Lord saved Sri-Gupta from spite and crime
And shewed how mercy conquers ev'n a foe,
And thus he taught Forgiveness' rule sublime,
To free his followers from the world and woe.

---

* Living beings are born as inanimate things by the law of *Karma* and vice versa.

† *Buddha, Dharma and Sangha,* Vide st. 73 above.

বিজ্ঞাপন।

IMPORTANT TO ALL LOVERS OF BENGALI LITERATURE.

রঘুবংশ।

(শ্রীনবীনচন্দ্র দাস, এম, এ, কর্ত্তৃক বাঙ্গালা পদ্যে অবিকল অনুবাদ।)

প্রথম ভাগ (১—৮ সর্গ) দিলীপ, রঘু ও অজের উপাখ্যান।
মূল্য ।৷৶০ আনা।

দ্বিতীয় ভাগ (৯—১৫ সর্গ) দশরথ ও রাম। মূল্য ১৲ টাকা।

তৃতীয় ভাগ (১৬—১৯ সর্গ) গ্রন্থ সমাপ্ত, কুশ হইতে অগ্নিবর্ণ পর্য্যন্ত রাজগণের বিবরণ। মূল্য ।৷৶০ আনা।

৩ খণ্ড একত্রে, কাপড়ের বাঁধাই, স্বর্ণাক্ষরযুক্ত। ২৲ টাকা।

কালিদাসের অমৃতময়ী লেখনী-প্রস্তুত সীতার বনবাস ও রামের স্বর্গারোহণ পাঠে আর্য্য-সন্তান মাত্রেরই হৃদয় শোকে অভিভূত হইবে।

RAGHU VAMSA.

(IN BENGALI VERSE.)

COMPLETE IN 3 PARTS.

BY

NOBIN CHANDRA DAS, M. A.

OF THE BENGAL PROVINCIAL SERVICE.

OPINIONS OF EMINENT PERSONS.

R. T. Griffith, Esq., M.A., C.I.E., translator of Rámáyana, Rig and Sam Vedas, late Principal of the Benares College, writes:—
"I am sure that your work will be welcomed by all who read it as a most valuable addition to Bengali poetic literature."
Kotágiri, *Nilgiri*, 21-1-95.

The Hon'ble Gooroo Das Banerjee, Judge of High Court, observed:—"...... I find that the translation is as faithful to the original as it is elegant and mellifluous."—*Calcutta*, 17th January, 1895.

The Hon'ble Mr. R. C. Dutt, C.S., C.I.E., writes:—"I recognized with pleasure the beauty of your style and the success of your undertaking. Your style is not only graceful and poetic but at the same time simple and easy, and herein lies the great merit of your performance......I hope your translations will be considered standard works."

Professor Krishna Kamal Bhattácharje, writes :—" I fully agree with the very favourable and eulogistic criticism that has been justly and deservedly elicited by your translation in every quarter. Your attempt to exhibit Kali Das in the garb of Bengali verse does credit to you, and must be pronounced successful. Translations in Bengali verse are generally unreadable : they are either unfaithful or crabbed in language. You have steered clear of both the dangers and have presented to the Bengali literature an excellent book of verse—of good, choice, readable and pleasing verse. This is a feat worthy of praise."—13*th April*, 1895.

The Hon'ble Dr. Rash Behary Ghose, Member of the Viceroy's Council, remarked :—" The translation has been well done and I have no hesitation in saying that you have rendered permanent service to the cause of Bengali literature."—27*th May*, 1892.

Mr. Satyendra Nath Tagore, C.S., Judge of Sholapur, Bombay, observed :—" The translation is excellent, the verses are sweet and easy, and the sense and beauty of the original are well preserved."—4*th June*, 1892.

Mr. Barada Charan Mitter, M.A., C.S., writes :—" It will be a permanent addition to Bengali literature. Your rendering is as chaste as it is accurate, and will be very welcome to readers ignorant of Sanskrit, but desirous of enjoying the beauties of Kali Dasa's poetry......Aja Bilap (canto 8) has really been very well rendered. Some of the stanzas are extremely pretty."

Babu Radha Nath Rai, Inspector of Schools, Orissa Division, remarked :—" The language is easy, graceful and flowing......the translator has brought to the task not only a thorough mastery of the Bengali tongue but also poetical gifts of a high order."—15*th June*, 1892.

Babu Akhil Chandra Sen, M.A., B.L., Vakil, Calcutta High Court, writes :—" I was really charmed with the book. It reads like an original and the sweet flow of the metre and the splendour of language will, I have no doubt, secure it a very high place in the literature of our country."

Babu Satis Chandra Vidyabhusan, M.A., Professor of Sanskrit, Krishnagar College, writes :—" Nobin Babu has presented the literary public with a very exquisite translation of Kali Dasa's Raghuvansa. While he has translated the slokas literally into Bengali verse, the beauty of the original has been fully preserved. The style is simple and elegant. The work may be selected as a suitable text-book for those candidates in the F. A. and Entrance Examinations who take up Bengali as their second language."—12*th January*, 1895.

Babu Nilkantha Mazumdar, Offg. Principal, Krishnagar College, writes :—" It gives me great pleasure to bear a willing testimony to the success with which your efforts have been crowned. Yours was a most difficult task. All good poets are untranslatable. But you have achieved an amount of success which has agreeably surprised me. Your translation is both literal and free, and what is more, you have to a great extent preserved the *spirit* of the original." 15*th August*, 1895.

Babu Nabin Chandra Sen, author of the "Battle of Plassey" "Kuru Kshetra," &c., writes :—" The translation *per se* is superb. You have by it laid the whole Bengali non-Sanskrit-knowing public, under deep obligation. The translation is so literal and at the same time so good, that in places it is nearly as good as the original. The imageries and the poetry of that great master of Sanskrit poetry have been wonderfully preserved. Indeed, it is impossible to speak of the translation too highly, displaying as it does, not only the mechanical hand of a translator, but that of a poet also."—*Calcutta*, 13*th May*, 1895.

OPINIONS OF THE PRESS.

"It is an excellent production and reflects great credit on the author, who has admirably succeeded in maintaining the beauty of the original in a true and literal translation of the great work of Káli Dása. The style is at once chaste, easy and graceful. The high sense of duty under which King Dilipa was ready to offer himself as a victim to the lion to save the life of Nandini, the divine cow, entrusted to his charge by the sage, Basistha, the munificence and heroism of Raghu and the civil virtues of Aja, and his love and sorrows for his fair consort, Indumati, whom he lost in the very bloom of her youth, depicted in such vivid colours by the inmitiable pen of Káli Dása, have been faithfully reproduced in Bengali, in the book before us. The 4th canto, describing the conquests of Raghu, and the 6th canto, with a charming account of the princes, assembled at the *Swayamvara Sabhá* of Indumati, in the capital of Bhoje Rájá, though rich in imagery, are full of interest to the reader as giving an idea of the geography and history of the times as known to Káli Dása and his contemporaries. The work, when completed, will undoubtedly be a valuable addition to Bengali literature."—"*The Statesman*," 7*th and* 22*nd June*, 1892.

"......The translator, while literally rendering the Slokas has preserved, as far as can be, the beauty of the original, and the language is easy and elegant."—" *The Englishman*," 23*rd February*, 1892.

Nobin Babu's book is a literal translation in Bengali verse of the greatest work of our immortal bard in a style which is at once easy, lucid and flowing. It has been freely urged by the anti-Bengali party that there are very few readable books in the field of Bengali literature. Nobin Babu's book, we are assured, will to a certain extent, remove the want......It is a source of pleasure to find that in a translation, which is at once so easy and literal, the beauty of the original has been so well kept up......we strongly draw the attention of the Education authorities to the book, which is undoubtedly fit to be a text-book in University Examinations."—"*Amrita Bazar Patrika*," 26-1-92.

"In our review of the first part we observed that Nobin Babu had a strong command over the Bengali language and possessed poetical gifts of a high order. It was qualities such as those which enabled him in preserving the thought, sentiment and beauty of description of the original in his translations in the present or in the first part. Indeed, in some respects the second part is an improvement over the first. Nobin Babu has inserted fuller notes in part second, explaining all the allusions and difficult ideas in the text, and has also given extracts from Mr. Griffith's translations in cantos xii, xiv and xv, thereby making easier for the ordinary reader, the immortal writings of our greatest Sanskrit bard. The style is simple, elegant and flowing."—"*Amrita Bazar Patrika*," 6th April, 1895.

A Bengali translation in verse of the first eight cantos of Raghu Vansa, by Babu Nobin Chandra Das, reflects great credit upon the writer......There is no doubt that he has succeeded to a great extent in giving us not only a metrical version of Raghu Vansa, but also a fair idea of the thought, sentiment and beauty of description that are to be found in the works of Káli Dása. The book will form an excellent addition to the text-books for the higher examinations in Bengali."—"*Hope*," 28th February, 1892.

The translation of Raghu Vansa into Bengali verse by Babu Nobin Chandra Das, M.A., of the Subordinate Executive service, is a new departure in Bengali literature and one that deserves to be encouraged. The translation is really well done, and we commend it to all lovers of Bengali literature."—"*Indian Nation*," 25th January, 1892.

This is an admirable translation of the great work of Káli Dása and supplies what was hitherto a real want in Bengali literature. We are glad to find the author in his attempt to popularise the works of the great Sanskrit poet, has not only succeeded in preserving the beauty of the original as far as it could be, but has made the translation easy and intelligible to the ordinary Bengali reader. The language is at once simple, elegant and forcible. We want to see the second part of the work published as soon as possible."—*The "Indian Mirror*," 5th August, 1892.

"The translation is being made with admirable fidelity to the original, and in language quite in keeping with its dignity. Babu Nobin Chandra Das's translation, when completed, will take its place in the forefront of the vernacular literature of Bengal."—*The "Indian Mirror*," March 30th, 1895.

Mahámahopádhyáya Mahesh Chandra Nyáratna, C. I. E., writes :—আপনার গ্রন্থে লালিত্য, সরলতা প্রভৃতি কয়েকটী গুণ বিলক্ষণ দৃষ্ট হয়, ইহা পাঠ করিলে, অনুবাদ বলিয়া বোধ হয় না, যেন একটী নূতন পদ্য কাব্য রচনা করিয়াছেন, অথচ রঘুবংশের ভাব প্রায় সমুদায়ই ইহাতে রক্ষিত হইয়াছে।... দ্বিতীয় খণ্ডে টীকা দিয়া সাধারণের পড়িবার বিশেষ সুবিধা করিয়া দিয়াছেন। সংস্কৃতানভিজ্ঞ ব্যক্তির মূল রঘুবংশের অভিপ্রায় জানিবার এবং অল্পসংস্কৃতজ্ঞ ব্যক্তির রঘুবংশ পাঠের একটী উৎকৃষ্ট উপায় করিয়া দিয়াছেন। আপনাকে আশীর্বাদ করি, আপনি এই রূপ কাব্য রচনা করিয়া বঙ্গভাষার উন্নতি সাধন করুন। (মহামহোপাধ্যায় শ্রীযুক্ত মহেশচন্দ্র ন্যায়রত্ন সি, আই, ই। কাশীধাম ৫ই মে, ১৮৯৫।)

মহামহোপাধ্যায় শ্রীযুক্ত মধুসূদন স্মৃতিরত্ন লিখিয়াছেন —"আপনি মহাকাব্য রঘুবংশের পদ্যে অনুবাদ করিয়া বঙ্গীয় সাহিত্যের শ্রীবৃদ্ধি সাধন করিয়াছেন সন্দেহ নাই। এ রূপ প্রাঞ্জল অথচ সুললিত সর্বাঙ্গ-সুন্দর অনুবাদ বিশেষ গৌরবের বস্তু। অনুবাদে মূলগ্রন্থের ভাব যথাযথ রক্ষিত হইয়াছে।" কলিকাতা সংস্কৃত কালেজ, ৩রা জৈষ্ঠ, ১৩০২।

সংস্কৃত কলেজের অধ্যাপক শ্রীযুক্ত বীরেশ্বর চট্টোপাধ্যায় লিখিয়াছেন ;—"আপনার অনুবাদ দুই খণ্ডই আদ্যোপান্ত পড়িলাম, তৃতীয় খণ্ড পড়িবার জন্য উৎসুক রহিলাম, আপনার অনুবাদ কি সুন্দরই হইয়াছে! পড়িয়া যে কত আনন্দ লাভ করিয়াছি লিখিয়া প্রকাশ করিতে পারি না। আপনার ভাষা প্রসাদ-গুণ-সম্পন্ন ও সুললিত ; আর কালিদাসের ভাবও প্রায় অবিকল প্রকাশ করিয়াছেন দেখিয়া বাস্তবিকই বিস্মিত হইয়াছি। সুকবির হাতে না হইলে কাব্যের এ রূপ অনুবাদ কখনই সম্ভবে না। আপনি কালিদাসের রঘুবংশ বাঙ্গালায় অনুবাদ করিয়া আমাদের সাহিত্যের পুষ্টি সাধন করিয়াছেন, সন্দেহ নাই।" কলিকাতা, ২৬শে নবেম্বর, ১৮৯৫।

মহামহোপাধ্যায় শ্রীযুক্ত চন্দ্রকান্ত তর্কালঙ্কার লিখিয়াছেন ;
" সুখের বিষয়, আপনি বাঙ্গালা ভাষায় মহাকবির ভাব প্রকাশ করার বিষয়ে অনেক দূর অগ্রসর হইয়াছেন। আপনি বাঙ্গালা ভাষার অঙ্গে যে উজ্জ্বল অলঙ্কার পরাইলেন, তজ্জন্য বঙ্গবাসী আপনার

নিকট কৃতজ্ঞ থাকিবে।" কলিকাতা, সংস্কৃত কলেজ। ৩১।৭।৯৫।

কবিবর রবীন্দ্রনাথ ঠাকুর লিখিয়াছেন,—সংস্কৃত কাব্যের এ রূপ প্রাঞ্জল এবং সুন্দর অনুবাদ দুর্লভ, আপনার অনুবাদে মূল গ্রন্থের ভাব সৌন্দর্য্য যথাসম্ভব রক্ষিত হইয়াছে।"

৵ কবিবর রাজকৃষ্ণ রায়—"আপনি বাঙ্গালা ভাষাকে যত্ন করিয়া একটী অত্যুজ্জ্বল অনুবাদ রত্ন প্রদান করিলেন, অতএব আপনি আমাদের সকলেরই বিশেষ ধন্যবাদার্হ। আমি আশা করি আপনি এই রূপ সরল সুন্দর বাঙ্গালা পদ্যে সমস্ত রঘুবংশ খানি অনুবাদ করিবেন।" ৬ই আশ্বিন, ১২৯৯।

প্রেসিডেন্সি কলেজের সহকারী সংস্কৃতাধ্যাপক শ্রীহরিশচন্দ্র কবিরত্ন লিখিয়াছেন;—"অদ্য আপনার এই পদ্যানুবাদ দেখিয়া আমি পরম প্রীতি লাভ করিলাম, ইহার ভাষা অতি প্রাঞ্জল এবং রচনা প্রণালী ও কবিত্ব-বোধিনী হইয়াছে। কালিদাসের ভাব গুলি প্রকাশ করিতে আপনি বিশেষ প্রয়াস পাইয়াছেন, এবং অনেক স্থলেও কৃতকার্য্য হইয়াছেন, ফলতঃ কোন ভাষা ভাষান্তরে পরিবর্ত্তিত করিলে, পূর্বভাষার ভাব গুলি পর ভাষায় সম্পূর্ণ প্রকাশ করা নিতান্ত কঠিন, স্থল বিশেষে অসম্ভব বলিলেও চলে, কিন্তু সুখের বিষয় আপনি অনেক স্থলেই মূল ভাব গুলি অবিকল কবিতাবদ্ধ করিতে সমর্থ হইয়াছেন।" কলিকাতা, ১৮ই এপ্রেল, ১৮৯৫।

শ্রীযুক্ত অনাথবন্ধু গুহ, বি, এল, (Vakil, Mymensing,) লিখিয়াছেন—"আপনি বাস্তবিকই বঙ্গ ভাষায় একটী নূতন রত্ন সংযোগ করিয়াছেন। আমাদিগের পরবর্ত্তিগণ এই রত্নের মূল্য বুঝিবে এবং সময়ের সঙ্গে সঙ্গে তাহার উজ্জ্বলতা বৃদ্ধি হইবে। আপনার অনুবাদের কোন কোন অংশ আমি মূলের সহিত মিলাইয়াছি; মূল অক্ষুন্ন রাখিয়া অনুবাদে এই প্রকার সৌন্দর্য্য বিকীর্ণ করা সামান্য ক্ষমতার কথা নহে।" ১৮ই জৈষ্ঠ, ১২৯৯।

"আপনার অনুবাদ যে অতি উৎকৃষ্ট হইয়াছে তাহা বলা নিষ্প্রয়োজন। পদ্যে এইরূপ অবিকল ও সৌন্দর্য্য রক্ষা করিয়া অনুবাদ অতি অল্প পুস্তকেরই হইয়াছে।" শ্রীরাজেশ্বর গুপ্ত (চট্টগ্রাম নর্ম্মাল স্কুলের হেড মাষ্টার)।

৬/০

ভূতপূর্ব "বান্ধব" সম্পাদক শ্রীযুক্ত কালীপ্রসন্ন ঘোষ লিখিয়া-ছেন ;—"আপনি রঘুবংশের এই পদ্যানুবাদ প্রকাশ করিয়া বাঙ্গালা সাহিত্যকে অলঙ্কৃত করিয়াছেন। অনুবাদ সরল হইলে সাধারণতঃ সুন্দর হয় না। অর্থ রক্ষার অনুরোধে আক্ষরিক হইলে, অন্যান্য অংশে প্রায় কখনও উপাদেয় হয় না। কিন্তু আপনার এ অনুবাদ সরল অথচ সুন্দর, আক্ষরিক অথচ উপাদেয়। বস্তুতঃ কাব্যের এই রূপ অনুবাদ যার পর নাই প্রশংসনীয় এবং ভাষার উপর অসাধারণ ক্ষমতার পরিচায়ক। এ পুস্তক দুখানি বিশ্ববিদ্যালয়ের প্রথম পরীক্ষায় "পাঠ্য" রূপে ব্যবহৃত না হইলে, তাহা বড়ই লজ্জা ও পরিতাপের কারণ হইবে।" ঢাকা, ৫ই আষাঢ়, ১৩০২।

সম্বাদ পত্রাদির মত।

"নবীন বাবু পদ্যে রঘুবংশের অনুবাদ করিয়া বাঙ্গালা ভাষার শ্রীবৃদ্ধি সম্পাদন করিয়াছেন। অতি স্খলিত ছন্দে নবীন বাবু মহা-কবির ভাব সম্পূর্ণরূপে বজায় রাখিয়া নিজে অনুবাদ করিয়াছেন, ইহা অল্প গৌরবের বিষয় নহে। আমাদের ধ্রুব জ্ঞান, অনুবাদ খানি সম্পূর্ণ হইলে উহা বাঙ্গালা ভাষায় এক খানি উজ্জ্বল অলঙ্কার স্বরূপ হইবে।" "সহচর" ১৭ই ফেব্রুয়ারি, ১৮৯২।

"নবীন বাবু এ বিষয়ে যে রূপ কৃতকার্য্য হইয়াছেন, তাহাতে তাঁহার ক্ষমতার প্রশংসা না করিয়া থাকিতে পারি না, গ্রন্থখানি সুপাঠ্য হইয়াছে, ইহা সম্পূর্ণাকারে প্রকাশিত দেখিবার প্রতীক্ষায় রহিলাম।" "বামাবোধিনী পত্রিকা," ফেব্রুয়ারি, ১৮৯২।

"আমরা ইতিপূর্বে ইহার প্রথম ভাগের সমালোচনা করিয়া গ্রন্থ-কারকে যে অন্তরের ধন্যবাদ দিয়াছি, এ বারে তাহা আরও শত গুণে না দিয়া থাকিতে পারি না, মহাকবি কালিদাসের অতুলনীয় গ্রন্থ বঙ্গীয় পরিচ্ছদে শোভাহীন হয় নাই এ কথা আমরা মুক্তকণ্ঠে বলিতে পারি। যে রূপ স্খলিত কবিতায় অনুবাদ সম্পন্ন হইয়াছে, তাহাতে ইহা অনুবাদ বলিয়াই বোধ হয় না, আমাদের প্রিয় কবির কবিত্বের ইহা সামান্য প্রমাণ নহে, উদ্ধৃত কবিতাদি সংযোগে গ্রন্থখানি আরও উপা-দেয় হইয়াছে।" "বামাবোধিনী পত্রিকা," মার্চ, ১৮৯৫।

"অনুবাদ স্খলিত ও অবিকল হইয়াছে, অমর কবি কালিদাসের উৎকৃষ্ট মহাকাব্য রঘুবংশের এ রূপ সর্ব্বাঙ্গ-সুন্দর অনুবাদ আমাদের বিশেষ আদরের জিনিষ।" "হিতবাদী," ১৭ই ফেব্রুয়ারি, ১৮৯২।

"এই খণ্ডে রঘুচরিত মাত্র আছে। কালিদাসের ভাব রক্ষা করিয়া অনুবাদ করা বড়ই কঠিন, এবং সেই কঠিন বিষয়ে যিনি কৃতকার্য্য হইতে পারেন, তিনিই প্রশংসার যোগ্য, নবীন বাবু এই দুরূহ অনুবাদ কার্য্যে কৃতকার্য্য হইয়াছেন, ইহাই তাঁহার প্রশংসা।" "হিতবাদী," ১৫।২।৯৫।

"নবীন বাবু মাতৃ-ভাষার সে অভাব দূরীকরণে কৃতসঙ্কল্প হইয়া দেশীয় বন্ধুবান্ধব ও পণ্ডিতমণ্ডলীর কৃতজ্ঞতাভাজন হইয়াছেন। সমস্ত ভাব ঠিক রাখিয়া ভাষান্তরে অনুবাদ করা বড় দুরূহ ব্যাপার। কিন্তু দুরূহ ব্যাপার হইলেও নবীন বাবু অকৃতকার্য্য হয়েন নাই, আশ্চর্য্যের বিষয় এই যে, প্রতি শব্দে শব্দে অনুবাদ করিতে গিয়াও নবীন বাবুর রসভঙ্গ ও মাধুর্য্যচ্যুতি ঘটে নাই। আমাদের মতে পুস্তক খানি পাঠ্য লিষ্টভুক্ত হওয়া আবশ্যক, বাঙ্গালা ছাত্রবৃত্তির পাঠ্যরূপে নির্ব্বাচিত হইলে ভাল হয়।" "সংশোধিনী," ৪ঠা ডিসেম্বর, ১৮৯১।

"এই পুস্তকের...অনুবাদ মনোহর হইয়াছে। গ্রহকার অতি সুললিত ভাষায় মহাকবি কালিদাসের কবিতা অনুবাদ করিয়াছেন, সংস্কৃতানভিজ্ঞ বঙ্গীয় পাঠকের নিকট এ পুস্তক আদৃত হইবে।" "সময়" ১।৪।৯২।

"অনুবাদ সরল, মধুর ও যথাযথ হইয়াছে...নবীন বাবু সুকবি, তাঁহার নিকট আমরা বঙ্গভাষার অনেক উন্নতির আশা করি।" "প্রকৃতি।"

"এ গ্রন্থে নবীন কবি অনেকাংশে কৃতকার্য্যও হইয়াছেন। অনেক স্থান পড়িয়া দেখিয়াছি, অনুবাদ যথাযথ ও প্রাঞ্জল হইয়াছে। সংস্কৃতানভিজ্ঞ পাঠকের পক্ষে ইহা বেশ সুবিধাজনক।" "নব্য-ভারত" পৌষ, ১২৯৮।

"আমরা নবীন বাবুর রঘুবংশের পদ্যানুবাদের দ্বিতীয় ভাগ পাঠ করিয়া পরম সুখী হইয়াছি। ইহার প্রথম ভাগ খানি অতি সুন্দর হইয়াছিল। আদ্যন্ত পাঠ করিয়া দেখিলাম দ্বিতীয় ভাগ খানি আরও সুন্দর হইয়াছে। নবীন বাবু অতি সুললিত ভাষায় মনোহর ছন্দে মহাকবির ভাব বজায় রাখিয়া বাঙ্গালা ভাষায় যে রঘুবংশের শেষাংশের অনুবাদ করিয়াছেন ইহা অল্প ক্ষমতার কার্য্য নহে। ফলতঃ নবীন বাবু প্রকৃত প্রস্তাবে সুকবি, বিশ্ববিদ্যালয়ে এফ, এ, পরীক্ষায় বাঙ্গালা ভাষা প্রচলিত করিবার প্রস্তাব হইতেছে। অনেকে বলিয়া থাকেন এফ, এ, পরীক্ষায় বাঙ্গালা পরীক্ষা প্রচলিত হইলে পরীক্ষার্থীর পাঠার্থে পুস্তকের অভাব হইবে, যাহারা নবীন বাবুর রঘুবংশের অনুবাদ পাঠ

করিয়াছেন, তাঁহাদের এই সংস্কার দূরীভূত হইবে। এ রূপ সুন্দর উন্নত পদ্য কাব্য বিশ্ববিদ্যালয়ের প্রবেশিকা ও এফ, এ, পরীক্ষার্থ নির্দ্দিষ্ট না হইলে আমরা বড়ই দুঃখিত হইব, সংস্কৃত পুস্তক নির্ব্বাচিকা সভা আগামী বৎসরের প্রবেশিকা পরীক্ষার পুস্তক নির্ব্বাচনের সময় যেন নবীন বাবুর পুস্তকের কিয়দংশ পাঠ্য রূপে নির্দ্দিষ্ট করেন, অর্থাৎ ঢাকা, কলিকাতা, হুগলী প্রভৃতি ট্রেনিং স্কুল কয়টিতে পড়াইবার জন্য ইহা অপেক্ষা উপযুক্ততর অধিক দেখা যায় না, আমরা প্রার্থনা করি, নবীন বাবু দীর্ঘজীবী হইয়া নিরন্তর মাতৃ-ভাষার শোভা বর্দ্ধন করিতে থাকুন।" "সহচর" ৯ই জানুয়ারি, ১৮৯৫।

"বাঙ্গালা ভাষায় সংস্কৃত কাব্যগ্রন্থের অনুবাদ করা নিরতিশয় কঠিন কাজ ; কারণ, সংস্কৃত কবিতার শ্লোক গুলি ধাতুময় কারুকার্য্যের ন্যায় অত্যন্ত সংহত ভাবে গঠিত, বাঙ্গালা অনুবাদে তাহা বিশ্লিষ্ট এবং বিস্তীর্ণ হইয়া পড়ে। কিন্তু নবীন বাবুর রঘুবংশ অনুবাদ খানি পাঠ করিয়া আমরা বিশেষ প্রীতিলাভ করিয়াছি, মূল গ্রন্থখানি পড়া না থাকিলেও এই অনুবাদের মাধুর্য্যে পাঠকদের হৃদয় আকৃষ্ট হইবে সন্দেহ নাই। অনুবাদক সংস্কৃত কাব্যের লাবণ্য বাঙ্গালা ভাষায় অনেকটা পরিমাণে সঞ্চারিত করিয়া দিয়াছেন ইহাতে তাঁহার যথেষ্ট ক্ষমতার পরিচয় পাওয়া যায়।" "সাধনা" বৈশাখ, ১৩০২।

সংস্কৃত মত।

Pandit Ajit Nath Nyayratna of Navadwipa, Commentator of "Nátya Parisista Vyákarana," writes :—

" কালিদাসকবিতাভ্র-গঙ্গয়া-
নীতনির্ম্মল-নবীন-পদ্যয়া ।
বঙ্গসাগর-সমুদ্বিধীর্ষয়া
গম্যতেঽদ্য সহ বঙ্গভাষয়া ॥"

নবদ্বীপনিবাসিনঃ ন্যায়রত্নোপাধিকশ্রীঅজিতনাথশর্ম্মণঃ।

Pandit Sitikantha Váchaspati of Navadwipa, writes :—

"आश्चर्यं रघुवंशभावसुफलं यत् कालिदास-द्रुमात्
सञ्जातं सुचिरं तथापि तनुते माधुर्य्यपूर्णं रसम् ।
सर्व्वेषामपि वाञ्छतामसुलभं यद्दुर्गमलाद्भुतं
तल्लाभाय नवीनपद्धतिरसौ वङ्गानुवादोऽभवत् ॥१॥"

नवद्वीपनिवासिनो वाचस्पत्युपाधिकस्य श्रीसितिकण्ठ-शर्म्मणः ।

Pandit Siva Narayan Siromani, Professor, Sanskrit College, Calcutta, writes :—

".......... महाकवेः कालिदासस्य सुधामय-संस्कृतरचितं रुचिरतमं कविकुलहृदयरत्नं तत् रघुवंशं नवीनकविना श्रीयुक्त नवीनचन्द्रदास-महोदयेन भाषान्तरितमपि अनुवादकस्य केनापि अनुवादपाटवेन, कयापि प्रतिभया, केनचित् कविल्व-सुलभलालित्य-सम्पादकगुणविशेषेण नवीनरचित-वङ्गभाषा-यौवनोचित-श्रीमन्तमणिभूतं रघुवंशमिदं सर्व्वेषां पाठकानां हृदयमाकर्षति ।

भाषान्तरितेषु पुस्तकेषु पूर्व्वभाषारसास्वादो न क्वापि घटते । किन्तु प्रकृतिभूतसन्दर्भस्य रसभावादिवैकल्यविरहे विकृतिसन्दर्भः किमपि चमत्कारातिशयं विधत्ते । अतोऽस्मत् प्रार्थनीयमेतत् :—

"नवीनभावैर्विरचितान्य-श्रीभं
महाकवेस्तद् रघुवंशरत्नम् ।
क्रमप्रकर्षोन्मुख-वङ्गभाषा
नवीनमूर्तिं समलङ्करोतु" ॥   इति १० आषाढ़ ।

शिरोमण्युपाधिक-श्रीशिवनारायण-शर्म्मणः ।

Pandit Sivanath Váchaspati of Krishnaghar, Maharajah's *Tol*, writes :—

"बहुमतरघुकाव्यं नीतिपूर्णं रसाढ्यं
मधुर-सरल-वाचस्पत्य वङ्गानुवादः ।

"বুধগয়াসুখদাতা যৎকৃতঃ শ্রীনবীনঃ
অতিসুখচিরজীবঃ সোঽস্তু বাঞ্ছা মমৈষা ॥"
শ্রীত্রিভুবনাথবাচস্পতিশর্ম্মণঃ।

Pandit Akshaya Chandra Smritiratna, Krishnaghar Mahárájah's spiritual guide, writes :—

"নবীন-নীতং নিজবঙ্গভাষয়া-
ঽনবীন-নব্যাদৃতমত্র তাবকম্ ।
নবীনকাব্যং রঘুবংশবর্ণনং
নবীন পদ্যং মধুরং বভুব হ ॥
মূলানুরূপং রসভাবপূর্ণং
মুকৈরবায়ছেমিবাত্র কাব্যং ।
নবীনচন্দ্রেণ বিকাশ্যমানং
দৃষ্ট্বা মনোঽসীমসুখং সমাপ্তং ॥"

আশীর্ব্বাদ শ্রীঅক্ষয়চন্দ্র-স্মৃতিরত্নশর্ম্মণঃ
নবদ্বীপরাজগুরোঃ।

"জন্মভূমির" সমালোচনা।
(উদ্ধৃত।)

"রঘুবংশ" অমর কবি কালিদাসের উৎকৃষ্ট মহাকাব্য। নবীন বাবু সেই মহাকাব্য বঙ্গভাষায় অনুবাদ করিয়া, বঙ্গবাসীকে এক উজ্জ্বল রত্ন উপহার দিয়াছেন। সংস্কৃত কাব্যের এমন মনোহর অথচ অবিকল অনুবাদ প্রায় দেখা যায় না। যাঁহারা সংস্কৃত জানেন না, মহাকবির সে মহাকাব্য সম্যক্ উপলব্ধি করিয়া, তাহার মধুর রস আস্বাদনে তাঁহারা বঞ্চিত। তাঁহারা জানেন না, সংস্কৃত সাহিত্য-ভাণ্ডারে কি উজ্জ্বল রত্নরাজি বিরাজ করিতেছে! এই অনুবাদ পাঠ করিলে, তাঁহারা সে অমূল্য মণি-মাণিক্যের আভাস পাইবেন। বঙ্গভাষাকে বিবিধ

রত্নরাজিতে সাজাইতে যাঁহার প্রয়াস, তিনি চিরদিনই আমাদের ধন্যবাদের পাত্র। নবীন বাবু শিক্ষিত ও কৃতী; বড় সুন্দর বিষয়েই তিনি হস্তক্ষেপ করিয়াছেন এবং তাঁহার হস্তে মহাকবির সে মহাকাব্যের মর্য্যাদা রক্ষিত হইয়াছে।

সংস্কৃত সাহিত্যের অনেক অনুবাদ প্রকাশিত হইয়াছে। অনেক অনুবাদ পাঠ করিয়া মনে হইয়াছে, অনুবাদকের পরিশ্রম বৃথায় গিয়াছে। যাঁহারা সংস্কৃত জানেন না, সে অনুবাদ পাঠে, অশ্বত্থামার দুগ্ধের পরিবর্তে দুগ্ধবৎ পানীয় গ্রহণের ন্যায়, তাঁহারা কাব্যের সম্যক্‌ সৌন্দর্য্য উপভোগে বঞ্চিত হইয়াছেন। কিন্তু নবীন বাবু কৃত রঘুবংশের এই বঙ্গানুবাদ সে শ্রেণীর অনুবাদ নহে। দুই একটির পরিচয় দিতেছি।

প্রথম সর্গে, মহারাজ দিলীপ, রাণী সুদক্ষিণার সহিত বশিষ্ঠের আশ্রমে গমন করিতেছেন। সে পথের বর্ণনা অতি সুন্দর;—

"রথের ঘর্ঘরে ভাবি মেঘের গর্জ্জন
ঊর্দ্ধমুখে কেকা রবে গায় শিখিগণ
পুলকে ষড়্‌জ রাগে, করিয়া শ্রবণ
সুদক্ষিণা সহ রাজা আনন্দে মগন।

অদূরে দাঁড়ায়ে পথে হরিণ হরিণী,
নির্ভয়ে নেহারে রথ বিশাল নয়নে,
কৌতুকে সে আঁখি-শোভা দেখে রাজা রাণী
পরস্পর আঁখিসহ তুলনে দুজনে।"

ষষ্ঠ সর্গে, অজ রাজের সহিত ইন্দুমতীর মিলন বর্ণিত হইয়াছে। স্বয়ম্বর-সভায় বহুদেশ হইতে বহু রাজা সম্মিলিত হইয়াছেন। সুনন্দা একে একে সকলের পরিচয় দিতেছে, কিন্তু

"তোজের ভগিনী ইন্দুমতীর হৃদয়ে,
না পশিল সুনন্দার বচন মধুর;
পশে কি সুধাংশু অংশু নিশীথ-সময়ে
মুদিত কমলে, রবি-বিরহ-বিধুর?

> "যে যে রাজগণে ছাড়ি চলিলা যুবতী
> ডুবিল তাঁদের মুখ দুঃখের আঁধারে ;
> রাজ-পথে দীপ-শিখা নিশীথে যেমতি
> গেলে চলি, হর্ম্ম্যরাজি ডুবে অন্ধকারে !"

অজের সহিত ইন্দুমতীর মিলন হইল ;—

> " এক দিকে বর-পক্ষ প্রফুল্ল সভায়,
> অন্য দিকে রাজ-বৃন্দ বিষণ্ণ-হৃদয়,
> ফুটিলে কমল যথা সরসে উষায়
> বিষাদে যুদিত আঁখি কুমুদ-নিচয় !"

অষ্টম সর্গে, মহারাজ রঘু, পুত্রের প্রতি রাজ্যভার অর্পণ করিয়া বানপ্রস্থ ব্রত অবলম্বন করিলেন। সে কেমন ?—

> "সুর্য্যকুলাকাশে আহা কি শোভা উদয় !
> শমাশ্রমে অস্ত রঘু পূর্ণ-শশধর,
> অন্য দিকে স্বর্ণাসন সুমেরু উপর
> উদিত অরুণরূপে রঘুর তনয় !"

এক দিন মহারাজ অজ, রাণী ইন্দুমতীকে লইয়া উপবনে বিহার করিতেছিলেন, সেই সময় মুনিবর নারদ বিমান পথে যাইতেছিলেন। তাঁহার বীণায় পারিজাতমালা শোভা পাইতেছিল। সহসা বীণাচ্যুত হইয়া সেই পারিজাত, রাণী ইন্দুমতীর হৃদয়ে পতিত হইল। সেই কুসুমস্পর্শে ইন্দুমতীর প্রাণ বিয়োগ হইল। অজের করুণ বিলাপে উপবন পূর্ণ হইল ;—

> "সুকুমার পারিজাত-কুসুম প্রহারে
> পার হে বধিতে, বিধি, যদি অবলারে,
> কোন্ দ্রব্যে ইচ্ছা তব না হয় সাধন,
> সংহার করিতে তব বাসনা যখন ?"

এমন আকুল ক্রন্দনে এই অষ্টম সর্গ পূর্ণ। "অজ-বিলাপ" অতি সুন্দর ও মধুর। উদ্ধৃত অংশ টুকু অনুবাদ বলিয়া মনে হয় কি ?

ইন্দুমতীর বিরহে শোকাতুর রাজা চারি দিকেই প্রিয়তমাকে দেখিতে-
ছেন। মৃতা পত্নীকে বলিতেছেন,—

"বায়ু-কোলে দোলে লতা, নিকুঞ্জ ভিতর,
বিলাস-বিভঙ্গ সে কি হরিল তোমার ?
কোকিলা হরিয়া তব কলকণ্ঠ স্বর
দিতেছে দ্বিগুণ ব্যথা চিত্তে অভাগার ;
হরিণী হরিল চারু চঞ্চল দর্শন,
কলহংসী হরিয়াছে মন্থর গমন !"

দুঃখ রহিল, সকল স্থান উদ্ধৃত করিতে পারিলাম না।
রাবণ বিনাশের পর, রামচন্দ্র সীতাকে লইয়া অযোধ্যায় ফিরিতে-
ছেন। ত্রয়োদশ সর্গে তাহাই বর্ণিত হইয়াছে। পথে আসিতে আসিতে
রামচন্দ্র এক এক সীতাকে নানা শোভা দেখাইতেছেন। সে বর্ণনার
সৌন্দর্য্যে রঘুবংশের ত্রয়োদশ সর্গ অতি অপূর্ব্ব হইয়াছে। ইংরাজিতে
সমুদ্রের বর্ণনা পড়িয়াছি, কিন্তু এমন মনোহারিত্ব কোথাও আছে কি ?—

"অপূর্ব্ব প্রেমের খেলা খেলেন সাগর,—
শত মুখে নদীকুল চুম্বিছে তাঁহারে,
প্রদানি তাদের মুখে তরঙ্গ-অধর
চতুর সরিত্-পতি তোষেন সবারে।"

রথ মেঘের পথ দিয়া আসিতেছিল। সীতা কৌতুকে রথের ভিতর
হইতে মেঘ স্পর্শ করিতে হস্ত প্রসারণ করিতেছেন, সহসা বিদ্যুৎ
আসিয়া সীতার করস্পর্শ করিতেছে। রামচন্দ্র বলিতেছেন,—

"যবে তুমি কুতূহলে রথ-বাতায়নে
প্রসারিছ কর, দেবি, পরশিতে ঘনে,
বারিদ আনিয়া নিজ বিজলী-বলয়
পরাইছে করে যেন, ক্ষণ-তেজোময় !"

তার পর নানা স্থান দেখাইতে দেখাইতে, রামচন্দ্র গঙ্গা-যমুনার
অপূর্ব্ব সঙ্গম স্থলে উপস্থিত হইলেন। সীতাকে সেই গঙ্গা-যমুনার
অপূর্ব্ব মিলন-শোভা দেখাইতেছেন ;—

"সুনীল যমুনা-জলে মিলি কুতূহলে
বহিছেন ওই শ্বেত সুর-তরঙ্গিনী —
মুক্তাহারে গাঁথা যেন ইন্দ্রনীলমণি,
শ্বেত-পদ্মমালা কিম্বা নীল-উৎপলে।

মানসের হংসরাজি ধবল-বরণা
নীল-হংসদলে যেন হ'য়েছে মিলিত,
ভূতলে চিত্রিত শ্বেতচন্দন-রচনা —
শোভে যেন কৃষ্ণপত্রে অগুরু-অঙ্কিত!

কোথাও জোছনা-জাল যেন রে চিত্রিত
স্থানে স্থানে ছায়া-লীন তিমির-পটলে,
কোথাও বা শরদের শুভ্র অভ্র দলে
ভেদি, যেন নীলাকাশ হ'তেছে লক্ষিত!

ধবল ভবেশ-অঙ্গ বিভূতি-ভূষিত
রহিয়াছে যেন কৃষ্ণ ভুজঙ্গে বেষ্টিত —
এ রূপে কতই রূপ হের, বরাননে,
ধরেন জাহ্নবী মিলি যমুনার সনে।

এ হেন সঙ্গম-স্থলে গঙ্গা-যমুনার,
তত্ত্বজ্ঞান অভাবেও যদি কোন জন
অবগাহি দেহ, হয় সুপবিত্র-মন,
মরণে না হয় তার জন্ম পুনর্ব্বার।"

অমর কবির সর্ব্বভেদিনী প্রতিভা সর্ব্বত্রই এমন সৌন্দর্য্য ঢালিয়া গিয়াছে! নবীন বাবুর বঙ্গানুবাদেও সেই সৌন্দর্য্য ফুটিয়াছে। আমরা তাঁহার অনুবাদ পড়িয়া মুগ্ধ হইয়াছি। এখনও তাঁহার অনুবাদ সম্পূর্ণ হয় নাই, আমরা সাগ্রহে তাহার প্রতীক্ষা করিতেছি।" "জন্মভূমি" আষাঢ়, ১৩০২।

NOTICE.

INDIAN PANDITS IN THE LAND OF SNOW.

(A NEW DISCOVERY OF THE WORKS OF ANCIENT INDIANS IN TIBET AND CHINA.)

By " *the distinguished traveller,*"

SARAT CHANDRA DAS, C.I.E.

Extract from annual address delivered at the Asiatic Society of Bengal by its President, the Hon'ble Sir Charles Alfred Elliott, K.C.S.I. (7th February, 1894, p. 19). " In his ' Indian Pandits in the Land of Snow,' Babu Sarat Chandra Das has reprinted in a handy and popular form, several lectures and essays in which he has traced the narrative of the efforts of Indian Buddhist Missionaries in China and Tibet."

" We read also sometime ago, Babu Sarat Chandra's ' Indian Pandits in the Land of Snow,' a book which exhibits an amount of labour and faculty for antiquarian researches, which has most deservedly raised the author so high in the estimation not only of his own countrymen but of all European nations as well. May Heaven protect him to add further glory to the country!—" *Amrita Bazar Patrika*" (31st January, 1894).

Price, Re. 1.

আকাশ-কুসুম কাব্য।

শ্রীনবীনচন্দ্র দাস, এম, এ, বি, এল, প্রণীত।

"একটী যুবক ও বালিকা অকৃত্রিম প্রেমে বদ্ধ হইয়া এক স্রোতে জীবন ভাসাইবার আশা করিয়াছিলেন, পিতা ধনলোভে বালিকাকে অন্য পাত্রসাৎ করিলেন, প্রণয়ীদের আশা "আকাশ কুসুম" হইল, এই বিষয় লইয়া কাব্য রচিত, নবীন বাবুর এই বাল্য রচনায় তাঁহার কবিত্ব শক্তির পরিচয় পাওয়া যায়, ইহার সঙ্গে যে কয়েকটী ক্ষুদ্র কবিতা আছে, তাহা অতি সুন্দর।" বামাবোধিনী পত্রিকা। (৯।৭৩)

LEGENDS AND MIRACLES OF BUDDHA, SAKYA SINHA.

PART I,

TRANSLATED INTO ENGLISH VERSE FROM KSHEMENDRA'S AVADÁN KALPA-LATÁ.

By NOBIN CHANDRA DAS, M.A. B.L.   Price, 8 annas.

A Note on the Geography of Válmiki-Rámáyana.

By the same author.   Price, 8 annas.

To be had of S. K. LAHIRI & Co., 54 COLLEGE STREET.
And at 86/2, Jaun Bazar Street, Calcutta.

www.ingramcontent.com/pod-product-compliance
Lightning Source LLC
Chambersburg PA
CBHW020258090426
42735CB00009B/1141